Tertullian, Origen, and Cassian on Prayer

TERTULLIAN, ORIGEN, AND CASSIAN ON PRAYER

ESSENTIAL ANCIENT CHRISTIAN WRITINGS

———————

QUINTUS TERTULLIAN

ORIGEN ADAMANTIUS

JOHN CASSIAN

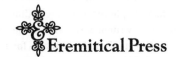

Eremitical Press

SURREY, BRITISH COLUMBIA

Tertullian, Origen, and Cassian on Prayer: Essential Ancient Christian Writings
Quintus Septimius Florens Tertullian (c. 160–c. 220)
Origen Adamantius (c. 185–254)
John Cassian (c. 360–435)
This edition copyright © 2011 Eremitical Press
This paper is acid free and meets all ANSI standards for archival quality paper.
ISBN 978-1-926777-26-9

Contents

Tertullian

On Prayer

CHAPTER 1

General introduction

The Spirit of God, and the Word of God, and the Reason of God; Word of Reason, and Reason and Spirit of Word; Jesus Christ our Lord, namely, who is both the one and the other, has determined for us, the disciples of the New Testament, a new form of prayer.

For in this particular also it was needful that new wine should be laid up in new skins, and a new breadth be sewn to a new garment (Matthew 9:16–17; Mark 2:21–22; Luke 6:36–37). Besides, whatever had been in bygone days has either been quite changed, as circumcision; or else supplemented, as the rest of the law; or else fulfilled, as prophecy; or else perfected, as faith itself. For the new grace of God has renewed all things from carnal unto spiritual by superinducing the Gospel, the obliterator of the whole ancient bygone system; in which our Lord Jesus Christ has been approved as the Spirit of God, and the Word of God, and the Reason of God: the Spirit, by which he was mighty; the Word, by which he taught; the Reason, by which he came. So the prayer composed by Christ has been composed of three parts.

In speech (by which prayer is enunciated), in spirit (by which alone it prevails), even John had taught his disciples to pray. But all John's doings were laid as groundwork for Christ, until, when "he had increased"—just as the same John used to fore-announce "that it was needful" that "he should increase and himself decrease" (John 3:30)—the whole work of the forerunner passed over, together with his spirit itself, unto the Lord. Therefore, after what form of words John taught to pray is not extant, because earthly things have given place to heavenly. "He who is from the earth," says John, "speaks earthly things; and he who is here from the heavens speaks those things which he has seen" (John 3:31–32). And what is the Lord Christ's—as this method of praying is—that is not heavenly?

And so, blessed brethren, let us consider his heavenly wisdom: first, touching the precept of praying secretly, whereby he exacted man's faith, that he should be confident that the sight and hearing of Almighty God are present beneath roofs and extend even into the secret place; and required modesty in faith, that it should offer its religious homage to him alone, whom it believed to see and to hear everywhere. Further, since wisdom succeeded in the following precept, let it in like manner appertain unto faith and the modesty of faith, so that we do not think that the Lord must be approached with a train of words, who, we are certain, takes unsolicited foresight for his own. And yet that very brevity—and let this make for the third grade of wisdom—is supported on the substance of a great and blessed interpretation, and is as diffuse in meaning as it is compressed in words. For it has embraced not only the special duties of prayer—be it veneration of God or petition for man—but almost every discourse of the Lord, every record of his discipline; so that, in fact, in the prayer is comprised an epitome of the whole Gospel.

CHAPTER 2

The first clause

The prayer begins with a testimony to God and with the reward of faith when we say, "Our Father who art in the heavens." For (in so saying) we at once pray to God and commend faith, whose reward this appellation is. It is written, "To them who believed on him he gave power to be called sons of God" (John 1:12). However, our Lord very frequently proclaimed God as a Father to us; nay, even gave a precept "that we call no one on earth father, but the Father whom we have in the heavens" (Matthew 23:9).Aand so, in thus praying, we are likewise obeying the precept. Happy they who recognize their Father! This is the reproach that is brought against Israel, to which the Spirit attests heaven and earth, saying, "I have begotten sons, and they have not recognized me" (Isaiah 1:2). Moreover, in saying "Father," we also call him "God." That appellation is one both of filial duty and of power. Again, in the Father the Son is invoked; "for I," says he, "and the Father are One" (John 10:30). Nor is even our mother the Church passed by—if, that is, in the Father and the Son is recognized the mother, from whom arises the name both of Father and of Son. In one general term, then, or word, we both honor God, together with his own, and are mindful of the precept, and set a mark on such as have forgotten their Father.

CHAPTER 3

The second clause

The name of "God the Father" had been published to none. Even Moses, who had interrogated him on that very point, had heard a different name (Exodus 3:13–16). To us it has been revealed in the Son, for the Son is now the Father's new name. "I am come," says he, "in the Father's name" (John 5:43). And again, "Father, glorify your name" (John 12:28), and more openly, "I have manifested your name to men" (John 17:6). That name, therefore, we pray may "be hallowed." Not that it is becoming for men to wish God well, as if there were any other by whom he may be wished well, or as if he would suffer unless we do so wish. Plainly, it is universally becoming for God to be blessed in every place and time, on account of the memory of his benefits ever due from every man. But this petition also serves the turn of a blessing. Otherwise, when is the name of God not "holy," and "hallowed" through himself, seeing that, of himself, he sanctifies all others—he to whom that surrounding circle of angels do not cease to say, "Holy, holy, holy" (Isaiah 6:3; Revelation 4:8)? In like wise, therefore, we too—candidates for angelhood, if we succeed in deserving it—begin even here on earth to learn by heart, who strain hereafter to be raised unto God and the function of future glory.

So far, for the glory of God. On the other hand, for our own petition, when we say, "Hallowed be thy name," we pray this: that it may be hallowed in us who are in him, as well in all others for whom the grace of God is still waiting (Isaiah 30:18); that we may obey this precept, too, in "praying for all" (1 Timothy 2:1), even for our personal enemies (Matthew 5:44). And therefore with suspended utterance, not saying, "Hallowed be it in us," we say, "in all."

CHAPTER 4
The third clause

According to this model, we subjoin, "Thy will be done in the heavens and on the earth"; not that there is some power withstanding to prevent God's will being done, and we pray for him the successful achievement of his will; but we pray for his will to be done in all. For, by figurative interpretation of flesh and spirit, we are "heaven" and "earth"; albeit, even if it is to be understood simply, still the sense of the petition is the same, that in us God's will be done on earth, to make it possible, namely, for it to be done also in the heavens.

What, moreover, does God will, but that we should walk according to his discipline? We make petition, then, that he supply us with the substance of his will and the capacity to do it, that we may be saved both in the heavens and on earth; because the sum of his will is the salvation of them whom he has adopted. There is, too, that will of God which the Lord accomplished in preaching, in working, in enduring: for if he himself proclaimed that he did not his own, but the Father's will, without doubt those things which he used to do were the Father's will (John 6:38); unto which things, as unto exemplars, we are now provoked; to preach, to work, to endure even unto death. And we need the will of God, that we may be able to fulfill these duties.

Again, in saying, "Thy will be done," we are even wishing well to ourselves, in so far that there is nothing of evil in the will of God; even if, proportionably to each one's deserts, somewhat other is imposed on us. So by this expression we premonish our own selves unto patience. The Lord also, when he had wished to demonstrate to us, even in his own flesh, the flesh's infirmity, by the reality of suffering, said, "Father, remove this your cup"; and, remembering himself, added, "save that not my will, but yours be done" (Luke 22:42). Himself was the will and the power of the Father: and yet, for the demonstration of the patience which was due, he gave himself up to the Father's will.

CHAPTER 5
The fourth clause

"Thy kingdom come" has also reference to that whereto "thy will be done" refers—in us, that is. For when does God not reign, in whose hand is the heart of all kings (Proverbs 21:1)? But whatever we wish for ourselves we augur for him, and to him we attribute what from him we expect. And so, if the manifestation of the Lord's kingdom pertains unto the will of God and unto our anxious expectation, how do some pray for some protraction of the age, when the kingdom of God, which we pray may arrive, tends unto the consummation of the age? Our wish is that our reign be hastened—not our servitude protracted. Even if it had not been prescribed in the prayer that we should ask for the advent of the kingdom, we should, unbidden, have sent forth that cry, hastening toward the realization of our hope. The souls of the martyrs beneath the altar cry in jealousy unto the Lord, "How long, Lord, do you not avenge our blood on the inhabitants of the earth?" (Revelation 6:10). For, of course, their avenging is regulated by the end of the age. Nay, Lord, your kingdom come with all speed—the prayer of Christians the confusion of the heathen, the exultation of angels, for the sake of which we suffer, nay, rather, for the sake of which we pray!

CHAPTER 6
The fifth clause

But how gracefully has the Divine Wisdom arranged the order of the prayer; so that after things heavenly—that is, after the "name" of God, the "will" of God, and the "kingdom" of God—it should give earthly necessities also room for a petition! For the Lord had withal issued his edict, "Seek ye first the kingdom, and then even these shall be added" (Matthew 6:33), albeit we may rather understand, "Give us this day our daily bread," spiritually. For Christ is our Bread; because Christ is Life, and bread is life. "I am," says he, "the Bread of Life" (John 6:35); and, a little above, "The Bread is the Word of the living God, who came down from the heavens" (John 6:33). Then we find, too, that his body is reckoned in bread: "This is my body" (Matthew 26:26). And so, in petitioning for "daily bread," we ask for perpetuity in Christ, and indivisibility from his body. But because that word is admissible in a carnal sense too, it cannot be so used without the religious remembrance withal of spiritual discipline; for the Lord commands that bread be prayed for, which is the only food necessary for believers; for "all other things the nations seek after" (Matthew 6:32). The like lesson he both inculcates by examples and repeatedly handles in parables, when he says, "Does a father take away bread from his children and hand it to dogs?" (Matthew 15:26; Mark 7:27). And again, "Does a father give his son a stone when he asks for bread?" (Matthew 7:9; Luke 11:11). For he thus shows what it is that sons expect from their father. Nay, even that nocturnal knocker knocked for "bread" (Luke 11:5–9). Moreover, he justly added, "Give us this day," seeing he had previously said, "Take no careful thought about the morrow, what you are to eat" (Matthew 6:34; Luke 12:29). To which subject he also adapted the parable of the man who pondered on an enlargement of his barns for his forthcoming fruits, and on seasons of prolonged security; but that very night he dies (Luke 12:16–20).

CHAPTER 7
The sixth clause

It was suitable that, after contemplating the liberality of God, we should likewise address his clemency. For what will aliments profit us if we are really consigned to them, as it were a bull destined for a victim? The Lord knew himself to be the only guiltless One, and so he teaches that we beg "to have our debts remitted us." A petition for pardon is a full confession; because he who begs for pardon fully admits his guilt. Thus, too, penitence is demonstrated acceptable to God who desires it rather than the death of the sinner (Exodus 18:23, 32; 33:11). Moreover, debt is, in the Scriptures, a figure of guilt; because it is equally due to the sentence of judgment, and is exacted by it: nor does it evade the justice of exaction, unless the exaction be remitted, just as the lord remitted to that slave in the parable his debt (Matthew 18:21–35); for hither does the scope of the whole parable tend. For the fact withal that the same servant, after liberated by his lord, does not equally spare his own debtor, and being on that account impeached before his lord, is made over to the tormentor to pay the uttermost farthing—that is, every guilt, however small—corresponds with our profession that "we also remit to our debtors"; indeed elsewhere, too, in conformity with this form of prayer, he says, "Remit, and it shall be remitted you" (Luke 6:37). And when Peter had put the question whether remission were to be granted to a brother seven times, "Nay," says he, "seventy-seven times" (Matthew 18:21–22) in order to remold the Law for the better; because in Genesis vengeance was assigned "seven times" in the case of Cain, but in that of Lamech "seventy-seven times" (Genesis 4:15, 24).

CHAPTER 8
The seventh or final clause

For the completeness of so brief a prayer he added—in order that we should supplicate not touching the remitting merely, but touching the entire averting, of acts of guilt—"Lead us not into temptation": that is, suffer us not to be led into it, by him (of course) who tempts; but far be the thought that the Lord should seem to tempt (James 1:13), as if he either were ignorant of the faith of any, or else were eager to overthrow it. Infirmity and malice are characteristics of the devil. For God had commanded even Abraham to make a sacrifice of his son, for the sake not of tempting, but proving, his faith; in order through him to make an example for that precept of his, whereby he was, by and by, to enjoin that he should hold no pledges of affection dearer than God. He himself, when tempted by the devil, demonstrated who it is that presides over and is the originator of temptation (Matthew 4:10; Luke 4:8). This passage he confirms by subsequent ones, saying, "Pray that you be not tempted" (Luke 22:40; Matthew 26:41; Mark 14:31); yet they were tempted, as they showed by deserting their Lord, because they had given way rather to sleep than prayer. The final clause, therefore, is consonant, and interprets the sense of "Lead us not into temptation"; for this sense is, "But convey us away from the Evil One."

CHAPTER 9
Recapitulation

In summaries of so few words, how many utterances of the prophets, the Gospels, the apostles—how many discourses, examples, parables of the Lord, are touched on! How many duties are simultaneously discharged! The honor of God in the "Father"; the testimony of faith in the "name"; the offering of obedience in the "will"; the commemoration of hope in the "kingdom"; the petition for life in the "Bread"; the full acknowledgment of debts in the prayer for their "forgiveness"; the anxious dread of temptation in the request for "protection." What wonder? God alone could teach how he wished himself prayed to. The religious rite of prayer therefore, ordained by himself, and animated, even at the moment when it was issuing out of the Divine mouth, by his own Spirit, ascends, by its own prerogative, into heaven, commending to the Father what the Son has taught.

CHAPTER 10
We pay add prayers of our own to the Lord's Prayer

Since, however, the Lord, the Foreseer of human necessities (Matthew 6:8), said separately, after delivering his rule of prayer, "Ask, and you shall receive" (Matthew 7:7; Luke 11:9); and since there are petitions which are made according to the circumstances of each individual; our additional wants have the right—after beginning with the legitimate and customary prayers as a foundation, as it were—of rearing an outer superstructure of petitions, yet with remembrance of the Master's precepts.

CHAPTER 11
When praying the Father, you are not to be angry with a brother

That we may not be as far from the ears of God as we are from his precepts, the memory of his precepts paves for our prayers a way unto heaven; of which precepts the chief is that we do not go up unto God's altar before we compose whatever of discord or offense we have contracted with our brethren (Matthew 5:22–23). For what sort of deed is it to approach the peace of God without peace? The remission of debts while you retain them? How will he appease his Father who is angry with his brother, when from the beginning "all anger" is forbidden us? For even Joseph, when dismissing his brethren for the purpose of fetching their father, said, "And be not angry in the way" (Genesis 45:24). He warned us, to be sure, at that time (for elsewhere our discipline is called "the way," Acts 9:2; 19:9, 23), that when set in "the way" of prayer, we do not go unto "the Father" with anger. After that, the Lord, "amplifying the Law" (Matthew 5:17), openly adds the prohibition of anger against a brother to that of murder (Matthew 5:21–22). Not even by an evil word does he permit it to be vented (1 Peter 3:9). If ever we must be angry, our anger must not be maintained beyond sunset, as the apostle admonishes (Ephesians 4:26). But how rash is it either to pass a day without prayer, while you refuse to make satisfaction to your brother; or else, by perseverance in anger, to lose your prayer?

CHAPTER 12

We must be free likewise from all mental perturbation

Nor merely from anger, but altogether from all perturbation of mind, ought the exercise of prayer to be free, uttered from a spirit such as the Spirit unto whom it is sent. For a defiled spirit cannot be acknowledged by a holy Spirit (Ephesians 4:30), nor a sad by a joyful (John 17:14; Romans 14:17), nor a fettered by a free (Psalm 51:12). No one grants reception to his adversary; no one grants admittance except to his compeer.

CHAPTER 13

Of washing the hands

But what reason is there in going to prayer with hands indeed washed, but the spirit foul? Inasmuch as to our hands themselves spiritual purities are necessary, that they may be "lifted up pure" (1 Timothy 2:8) from falsehood, from murder, from cruelty, from poisonings, from idolatry, and all the other blemishes which, conceived by the spirit, are effected by the operation of the hands. These are the true purities (Matthew 15:10,

11, 17–20; 23:25–26); not those which most are superstitiously careful about, taking water at every prayer, even when they are coming from a bath of the whole body. When I was scrupulously making a thorough investigation of this practice, and searching into the reason of it, I ascertained it to be a commemorative act, bearing on the surrender (Matthew 27:24) of our Lord. We, however, pray to the Lord: we do not surrender him; nay, we ought even to set ourselves in opposition to the example of his surrenderer, and not, on that account, wash our hands. Unless any defilement contracted in human intercourse be a conscientious cause for washing them, they are otherwise clean enough, which together with our whole body we once washed in Christ [in baptism].

CHAPTER 14
Apostrophe

Albeit Israel washed daily all his limbs over, yet is he never clean. His hands, at all events, are ever unclean, eternally dyed with the blood of the prophets and of the Lord himself; and on that account, as being hereditary culprits from their privity to their fathers' crimes (Matthew 23:31; Luke 11:48), they do not dare even to raise them unto the Lord, for fear some Isaiah should cry out (Isaiah 1:15), for fear Christ should utterly shudder. We, however, not only raise, but even expand them; and, taking our model from the Lord's passion even in prayer we confess to Christ.

CHAPTER 15
Of putting off cloaks

But since we have touched on one special point of empty observance, it will not be irksome to set our brand likewise on the other points against which the reproach of vanity may deservedly be laid; if, that is, they are observed without the authority of any precept either of the Lord, or else of the apostles. For matters of this kind belong not to religion, but to superstition, being studied, and forced, and of curious rather than rational ceremony; deserving of restraint, at all events, even on this ground, that they put us on a level with Gentiles. As, for example, it is the custom of some to make prayer with cloaks doffed, for so do the nations approach their idols; which practice, of course, were its observance becoming, the apostles, who teach concerning the garb of prayer (1 Corinthians 11:3–16), would have comprehended in their instructions, unless any think that it was in prayer that Paul had left his cloak with Carpus (2 Timothy 4:13)! God, forsooth, would not hear cloaked suppliants, who plainly heard the three saints in the Babylonian king's furnace praying in their trousers and turbans (Daniel 3:21, etc.).

CHAPTER 16

Of sitting after prayer

Again, for the custom which some have of sitting when prayer is ended, I perceive no reason, except that which children give. For what if that Hermas, whose writing is generally inscribed with the title *The Shepherd*, had, after finishing his prayer, not sat down on his bed, but done some other thing: should we maintain that also as a matter for observance? Of course not. Why, even as it is the sentence, "When I had prayed, and had sat down on my bed," is simply put with a view to the order of the narration, not as a model of discipline. Else we shall have to pray nowhere except where there is a bed! Nay, whoever sits in a chair or on a bench, will act contrary to that writing. Further, inasmuch as the nations do the like, in sitting down after adoring their petty images; even on this account the practice deserves to be censured in us because it is observed in the worship of idols. To this is further added the charge of irreverence—intelligible even to the nations themselves, if they had any sense. If, on the one hand, it is irreverent to sit under the eye, and over against the eye, of him whom you most of all revere and venerate; how much more, on the other hand, is that deed most irreligious under the eye of the living God, while the angel of prayer is still standing by unless we are upbraiding God that prayer has wearied us!

CHAPTER 17
Of elevated hands

But we more commend our prayers to God when we pray with modesty and humility, with not even our hands too loftily elevated, but elevated temperately and becomingly; and not even our countenance over-boldly uplifted. For that publican who prayed with humility and dejection not merely in his supplication, but in his countenance too, went his way "more justified" than the shameless Pharisee (Luke 18:9–14). The sounds of our voice, likewise, should be subdued; else, if we are to be heard for our noise, how large windpipes should we need! But God is the hearer not of the voice, but of the heart, just as he is its inspector. The demon of the Pythian oracle says, "And I do understand the mute, and plainly hear the speechless one." Do the ears of God wait for sound? How, then, could Jonah's prayer find way out unto heaven from the depth of the whale's belly, through the entrails of so huge a beast; from the very abysses, through so huge a mass of sea? What superior advantage will they who pray too loudly gain, except that they annoy their neighbors? Nay, by making their petitions audible, what less error do they commit than if they were to pray in public (Matthew 6:5–6)?

CHAPTER 18
Of the kiss of peace

Another custom has now become prevalent. Such as are fasting withhold the kiss of peace, which is the seal of prayer, after prayer made with brethren. But when is peace more to be concluded with brethren than when, at the time of some religious observance, our prayer ascends with more acceptability; that they may themselves participate in our observance, and thereby be mollified for transacting with their brother touching their own peace? What prayer is complete if divorced from the "holy kiss?" (Romans 16:16; 1 Corinthians 16:20; 2 Corinthians 13:12; 1 Thessalonians 5:26; 1 Peter 5:14). Whom does peace impede when rendering service to his Lord? What kind of sacrifice is that from which men depart without peace? Whatever our prayer be, it will not be better than the observance of the precept by which we are bidden to conceal our fasts (Matthew 6:16–18); for now, by abstinence from the kiss, we are known to be fasting. But even if there be some reason for this practice, still, lest you offend against this precept, you may perhaps defer your "peace" at home, where it is not possible for your fast to be entirely kept secret. But wherever else you can conceal your observance, you ought to remember the precept: thus you may satisfy the requirements of discipline abroad and of custom at home. So, too, on the day of the Passover [Good Friday], when the religious observance of a fast is general, and as it were public, we justly forego the kiss, caring nothing to conceal anything which we do in common with all.

CHAPTER 19
Of stations

Similarly, too, touching the days of stations [fasts], most think that they must not be present at the sacrificial prayers, on the ground that the station must be dissolved by reception of the Lord's Body. Does, then, the Eucharist cancel a service devoted to God, or bind it more to God? Will not your station be more solemn if you have withal stood at God's altar? When the Lord's Body has been received and reserved, each point is secured, both the participation of the sacrifice and the discharge of duty. If the "station" has received its name from the example of military life—for we withal are God's military (2 Timothy 2:1)—of course no gladness or sadness chanting to the camp abolishes the "stations" of the soldiers: for gladness will carry out discipline more willingly, sadness more carefully.

CHAPTER 20
Of women's dress

So far, however, as regards the dress of women, the variety of observance compels us—men of no consideration whatever—to treat, presumptuously indeed, after the most holy apostle (1 Corinthians 11:1–16; 1 Timothy 2:9–10), except in so far as it will not be presumptuously if we treat the subject in accordance with the apostle. Touching modesty of dress and ornamentation, indeed, the prescription of Peter (1 Peter 3:1–6) likewise is plain, checking as he does with the same mouth, because with the same Spirit, as Paul, the glory of garments, and the pride of gold, and the meretricious elaboration of the hair.

CHAPTER 21
Of virgins

But that point which is promiscuously observed throughout the churches, whether virgins ought to be veiled or no, must be treated of. For they who allow to virgins immunity from head-covering, appear to rest on this: that the apostle has not defined "virgins" by name, but "women" (1 Corinthians 11:5) as "to be veiled"; nor the sex generally, so as to say "females," but a class of the sex, by saying "women." For if he had named the sex by saying "females," he would have made his limit absolute for every woman; but while he names one class of the sex, he separates another class by being silent. For, they say, he might either have named "virgins" specially; or generally, by a compendious term, "females."

CHAPTER 22

Answer to the foregoing arguments

They who make this concession ought to reflect on the nature of the word itself—what is the meaning of "woman" from the very first records of the sacred writings. Here they find it to be the name of the sex, not a class of the sex: if, that is, God gave to Eve, when she had not yet known a man, the surname "woman" and "female" (Genesis 2:23)—"female," whereby the sex generally; "woman," hereby a class of the sex, is marked. So, since at that time the as yet unwedded Eve was called by the word "woman," that word has been made common even to a virgin. Nor is it wonderful that the apostle—guided, of course, by the same Spirit by whom, as all the divine Scripture, so that book Genesis was drawn up—has used the selfsame word in writing "women," which, by the example of Eve unwedded, is applicable too to a "virgin."

In fact, all the other passages are in consonance herewith. For even by this very fact, that he has not named "virgins"—as he does in another place (1 Corinthians 7:34) where he is teaching touching marrying—he sufficiently predicates that his remark is made touching every woman, and touching the whole sex; and that there is no distinction made between a "virgin" and any other, while he does not name her at all. For he who elsewhere—namely, where the difference requires—remembers to make the distinction (moreover, he makes it by designating each species by their appropriate names), wishes, where he makes no distinction (while he does not name each), no difference to be understood.

What of the fact that in the Greek speech, in which the apostle wrote his letters, it is usual to say "women" rather than "females"; that is, *gunaikas* rather than *theleias*? Therefore if that word, which by interpretation represents what "female" (*femina*) represents, is frequently used instead of the name of the sex, he has named the sex in saying *gunaika*; but in the sex even the virgin is embraced. But, withal, the declaration is plain: "Every woman," says he, "praying and prophesying with head uncovered, dishonors her own head" (1 Corinthians 11:5). What is "every woman," but woman of every age, of every rank, of every condition? By saying "every" he excepts nought of womanhood, just as he excepts nought of manhood either from not being covered; for just so he says, "every man" (1 Corinthians 11:4). As, then, in the masculine sex, under the name of "man" even the "youth" is forbidden to be veiled; so, too, in the feminine, under the name of "woman," even the "virgin" is bidden to be veiled.

Equally in each sex let the younger age follow the discipline of the elder; or else let the male "virgins," too, be veiled, if the female virgins withal are not veiled, because they are not mentioned by name. Let "man" and "youth" be different, if "woman" and "virgin" are different. For indeed it is "on account of the angels" (1 Corinthians 11:10) that he says women must be veiled, because on account of "the daughters of men" angels revolted from God. Who then, would contend that "women" alone— that is, such as were already wedded and had lost their virginity—were the objects of angelic concupiscence, unless "virgins" are incapable of excelling in beauty and finding lovers? Nay, let us see whether it were not virgins alone whom they lusted after; since Scriptures says, "the daughters of men" (Genesis 4:2), inasmuch as it might have named "wives of men," or "females," indifferently. Likewise, in that it says, "And they took them to themselves for wives" (Genesis 6:2), it does so on this ground, that, of course, such are "received for wives" as are devoid of that title. But it would have expressed itself differently concerning such as were not thus devoid. And so (they who are named) are devoid as much of widowhood as of virginity. So completely has Paul, by naming the sex generally, mingled "daughters" and species together in the genus.

Again, while he says that "nature herself" (1 Corinthians 11:14), which has assigned hair as a tegument and ornament to women, "teaches that veiling is the duty of females," has not the same tegument and the same honor of the head been assigned also to virgins? If "it is shameful" for a woman to be shorn, it is similarly so to a virgin, too. From them, then, to whom is assigned one and the same law of the head, one and the same discipline of the head is exacted—(which extends) even unto those virgins whom their childhood defends, for from the first a virgin was named "female." This custom, in short, even Israel observes; but if Israel did not observe it, our Law, amplified and supplemented, would vindicate the addition for itself; let it be excused for imposing the veil on virgins also.

Under our dispensation, let that age which is ignorant of its sex retain the privilege of simplicity. For both Eve and Adam, when it befell them to be "wise" (Genesis 3:6), forthwith veiled what they had learned to know (Genesis 2:27; 3:7, 10–11). At all events, with regard to those in whom girlhood has changed (into maturity), their age ought to remember its duties as to nature, so also, to discipline; for they are being transferred to the rank of "women" both in their persons and in their functions. No one is a "virgin" from the time when she is capable of marriage; seeing that, in her, age has by that time been wedded to its own husband, that is, to time.

"But some particular virgin has devoted herself to God. From that very moment she both changes the fashion of her hair, and converts all her garb into that of a 'woman.'" Let her, then, maintain the character wholly and perform the whole function of a "virgin": what she conceals for the sake of God, let her cover quite over.

It is our business to entrust to the knowledge of God alone that which the grace of God effects in us, lest we receive from man the reward we hope for from God. Why do you denude before God what you cover before men? Will you be more modest in public than in the church? If your self-devotion is a grace of God, and you have received it, "Why do you boast," says he, "as if you have not received it?" (1 Corinthians 4:7). Why, by your ostentation of yourself, do you judge others? Is it that, by your boasting, you invite others unto good? Nay, but even you yourself run the risk of losing, if you boast; and you drive others unto the same perils! What is assumed from love of boasting is easily destroyed. Be veiled, virgin, if virgin you are; for you ought to blush. If you are a virgin, shrink from (the gaze of) many eyes. Let no one wonder at your face; let no one perceive your falsehood. You do well in falsely assuming the married character, if you veil your head; nay, you do not seem to assume it falsely, for you are wedded to Christ: to him you have surrendered your body; act as becomes your Husband's discipline. If he bids the brides of others to be veiled, his own, of course, much more.

"But each individual man is not to think that the institution of his predecessor is to be overturned." Many yield up their own judgment, and its consistency, to the custom of others. Granted that virgins be not compelled to be veiled, at all events such as voluntarily are so should not be prohibited; who, likewise, cannot deny themselves to be virgins, content, in the security of a good conscience before God, to damage their own fame. Touching such, however, as are betrothed, I can with constancy "above my small measure" pronounce and attest that they are to be veiled from that day forth on which they shuddered at the first bodily touch of a man by kiss and hand. For in them everything has been forewedded: their age, through maturity; their flesh, through age; their spirit, through consciousness; their modesty, through the experience of the kiss their hope, through expectation; their mind through volition. And Rebecca is example enough for us, who, when her betrothed had been pointed out, veiled herself for marriage merely on recognition of him (Genesis 24:64–65).

CHAPTER 23
Of kneeling

In the matter of kneeling also, prayer is subject to diversity of observance, through the act of some few who abstain from kneeling on the Sabbath; and since this dissension is particularly on its trial before the churches, the Lord will give his grace that the dissentients may either yield, or else indulge their opinion without offense to others. We, however (just as we have received), only on the day of the Lord's Resurrection ought to guard not only against kneeling, but every posture and office of solicitude; deferring even our businesses lest we give any place to the devil

(Ephesians 4:27). Similarly, too, in the period of Pentecost; which period we distinguish by the same solemnity of exultation. But who would hesitate every day to prostrate himself before God, at least in the first prayer with which we enter on the daylight? At fasts, moreover, and stations, no prayer should be made without kneeling, and the remaining customary marks of humility; for (then) we are not only praying, but deprecating, and making satisfaction to God our Lord.

Touching times of prayer, nothing at all has been prescribed, except clearly "to pray at every time and every place" (Ephesians 6:18; 1 Thessalonians 5:17; 1 Timothy 2:8).

CHAPTER 24
Of Place for Prayer

But how "in every place," since we are prohibited (Matthew 6:5–6) from praying in public? In every place, he means, which opportunity or even necessity, may have rendered suitable: for that which was done by the apostles (Acts 16:25)—who, in jail, in the audience of the prisoners, "began praying and singing to God"—is not considered to have been done contrary to the precept; nor yet that which was done by Paul, who in the ship, in presence of all, "made thanksgiving to God."

CHAPTER 25
Of time for prayer

Touching the time, however, the extrinsic observance of certain hours will not be unprofitable—those common hours, I mean, which mark the intervals of the day—the third, the sixth, the ninth—which we may find in the Scriptures to have been more solemn than the rest. The first infusion of the Holy Spirit into the congregated disciples took place at "the third hour" (Acts 2:1–4, 14–15). Peter, on the day on which he experienced the vision of universal community, exhibited in that small vessel, had ascended into the more lofty parts of the house, for prayer's sake "at the sixth hour" (Acts 10:9). The same apostle was going into the temple, with John, "at the ninth hour" (Acts 3:1), when he restored the paralytic to his health. Albeit these practices stand simply without any precept for their observance, still it may be granted a good thing to establish some definite presumption, which may both add stringency to the admonition to pray, and may, as it were by a law, tear us out from our businesses unto such a duty; so that—what we read to have been observed by Daniel also (Daniel 6:10; cf. Psalm 55:17), in accordance, of course, with Israel's discipline—we pray at least not less than thrice in the day, debtors as we are to Three—Father, Son, and Holy Spirit: of course, in addition to our regular prayers which are due, without any admonition, on the entrance of light and of night.

But, withal, it becomes believers not to take food, and not to go to the bath, before interposing a prayer; for the refreshments and nourishments of the spirit are to be held prior to those of the flesh, and things heavenly prior to things earthly.

CHAPTER 26

Of the parting of brethren

You will not dismiss a brother who has entered your house without prayer—"Have you seen," says Scripture, "a brother? You have seen your Lord"—especially "a stranger," lest perhaps he be "an angel." But again, when received yourself by brethren, you will not make earthly refreshments prior to heavenly, for your faith will forthwith be judged. Or else how will you—according to the precept (Luke 10:5)—say, "Peace to this house," unless you exchange mutual peace with them who are in the house?

CHAPTER 27
Of subjoining a psalm

The more diligent in prayer are wont to subjoin in their prayers the "Hallelujah," and such kind of psalms, in the closes of which the company respond. And, of course, every institution is excellent which, for the extolling and honoring of God, aims unitedly to bring him enriched prayer as a choice victim (Hosea 14:2).

CHAPTER 28
Of the spiritual victim, which prayer is

For this is the spiritual victim (1 Peter 2:5) which has abolished the pristine sacrifices. "To what purpose," says he, "do you bring me the multitude of your sacrifices? I am full of holocausts of rams, and I desire not the fat of rams, and the blood of bulls and of goats. For who has required these from your hands?" (Isaiah 1:11).What, then, God has required, the Gospel teaches. "An hour will come," says he, "when the true adorers shall adore the Father in spirit and truth. For God is a Spirit, and accordingly requires his adorers to be such" (John 4:23–24). We are the true adorers and the true priests, who, praying in spirit (1 Corinthians 14:15; Ephesians 6:18), sacrifice, in spirit, prayer—a victim proper and acceptable to God, which assuredly he has required, which he has looked forward to for himself ! This victim, devoted from the whole heart, fed on faith, tended by truth, entire in innocence, pure in chastity, garlanded with love, we ought to escort with the pomp of good works, amid psalms and hymns, unto God's altar, to obtain for us all things from God.

CHAPTER 29
Of the power of prayer

For what has God, who exacts it, ever denied to prayer coming from "spirit and truth?" How mighty specimens of its efficacy do we read, and hear, and believe! Old-world prayer, indeed, used to free from fires (Daniel 3) and from beasts (Daniel 6), and from famine (1 Kings 18; James 5:17–18); and yet it had not (then) received its form from Christ. But how far more amply operative is Christian prayer! It does not station the angel of dew in mid-fires, nor muzzle lions, nor transfer to the hungry the rustics' bread (2 Kings 4:42–44); it has no delegated grace to avert any sense of suffering; but it supplies the suffering, and the feeling, and the grieving, with endurance: it amplifies grace by virtue, that faith may know what she obtains from the Lord, understanding what—for God's name's sake—she suffers. But in days gone by, withal prayer used to call down plagues, scatter the armies of foes, withhold the wholesome influences of the showers. Now, however, the prayer of righteousness averts all God's anger, keeps bivouac on behalf of personal enemies, makes supplication on behalf of persecutors. Is it wonder if it knows how to extort the rains of heaven—prayer which was once able to procure its fires (2 Kings 1)? Prayer is alone that which vanquishes God. But Christ has willed that it be operative for no evil: he had conferred on it all its virtue in the cause of good. And so it knows nothing save how to recall the souls of the departed from the very path of death, to transform the weak, to restore the sick, to purge the possessed, to open prison-bars, to loose the bonds of the innocent. Likewise it washes away faults, repels temptations, extinguishes persecutions, consoles the faint-spirited, cheers the high-spirited, escorts travelers, appeases waves, makes robbers stand aghast, nourishes the poor, governs the rich, upraises the fallen, arrests the falling, confirms the standing. Prayer is the wall of faith: her arms and missiles against the foe who keeps watch over us on all sides. And so we never walk unarmed. By day, we are mindful of station; by night, of vigil. Under the arms of prayer, we guard the standard of our General; we await in prayer the angel's trump (1 Corinthians 16:52; 1 Thessalonians 4:16). The angels, likewise, all pray; every creature prays; cattle and wild beasts pray and bend their knees; and when they issue from their layers and lairs, they look up heavenward with no idle mouth, making their breath vibrate after their own manner. Nay, the birds too, rising out of the nest, upraise themselves heavenward, and, instead of hands, expand the cross of their wings, and say somewhat to seem like prayer. What more then, touching the office of prayer? Even the Lord himself prayed; to whom be honor and virtue unto the ages of the ages!

Origen

On Prayer

CHAPTER 1
Introduction

Things in themselves so supremely great, so far above man, so utterly above our perishable nature as to be impossible for the race of rational mortals to grasp, as the will of God, became possible in the immeasurable abundance of the Divine grace which streams forth from God upon men, through Jesus Christ, the minister of his unsurpassable grace toward us, and through the cooperant Spirit. Thus, though it is a standing impossibility for human nature to acquire Wisdom, by which all things have been established—for all things, according to David, God made in wisdom—from being impossible it becomes possible through our Lord Jesus Christ, who was made for us wisdom from God and righteousness and sanctification and redemption.

For what or who is man that he shall know the counsel of God, or who shall conceive what that Lord wills? Since the thoughts of mortals are weakling, and our purposes are prone to fail; for the body that is corruptible weighs down the soul, and the mind with its store of thought is burdened by its earthly tabernacle; and things on earth we forecast with difficulty, but things in heaven, whoever yet traced out? Who would not say that it is impossible for man to trace out things in heaven? Yet this impossible thing, by the surpassing grace of God, becomes possible; for he who was caught up unto a third heaven traced out things in the three heavens through having heard unutterable utterances, which it was not permitted for man to speak. Who can say that it is possible for the mind of the Lord to be known by man?

But this, too, God graciously gives through Christ, who said to his disciples: "No longer do I call you servants, because the servant knows not what his lord's will is, but I have called you friends, because all the things that I have heard from my Father I have made known to you" (John 15:15); so that through Christ there is made known to them the will of one who, when he teaches them the will of the Lord, has no desire to be their lord any longer but instead becomes a friend to those whose lord he was before. Moreover, as no one knows the things of man save the Spirit of man that is in him, so also no one knows the things of God save the Spirit of God.

Now, if no one knows the things of God save the Spirit of God, it is impossible that a man should know the things of God. But mark how this too becomes possible: but we, he says, have received not the spirit of the world but the spirit which is from God, that we may know the things graciously given to us by God, and these also we speak not in words taught of human wisdom but in those taught of the Spirit. But I think, right pious and industrious Ambrosius, and right discreet and manful Tatiana, from whom I avow that womanly weakness has disappeared as truly as it had from Sarah of old, you are wondering to what purpose all this has been said in preface about things impossible for man becoming possible by the grace of God, when the subject prescribed for our discourse is Prayer.

The fact is, I believe it to be itself one of those things which, judged by our weakness, are impossible, clearly to set forth with accuracy and reverence a complete account of prayer, and in particular of how prayer ought to be offered, what ought to be said to God in prayer, which seasons are more, which less, suitable for prayer. . . . The very apostle who by reason of the abundance of the revelations is anxious that no one should account to him more than he sees or hears from him, confesses that he knows not how to pray as he ought; for what we ought to pray, he says, we know not how to as we ought (Romans 8:26). It is necessary not merely to pray but also to pray *as* we ought and to pray *what* we ought. For even though we are enabled to understand what we ought to pray, that is not adequate if we do not add to it the right manner also.

On the other hand, what is the use of the right manner to us if we do not know to pray for what we ought? Of these two things the one, I mean the "what we ought" of prayer, is the language of the prayer, while the "as we ought" is the disposition of him who prays. Thus the former is illustrated by "Ask for the great things, and the little shall be added unto you," and "Ask for the heavenly things, and the earthly shall be added unto you" (Matthew 6:33), and "Pray for them that abuse you" (Matthew 5:11), and "Entreat therefore the Lord of the harvest that he send out workers unto his harvest" (Matthew 9:38), and "Pray that you enter not into temptation" (Luke 22:40), and "Pray that your flight be not in winter or on a Sabbath" (Matthew 24:20), and "In praying babble not" (Matthew 6:7) and the like passages—the latter by "I desire therefore that men pray in every place, lifting up holy hands without anger and questioning, and in like manner that women array themselves decently in simplicity, with modesty and discretion, not in or gold or pearls or costly raiments, but, as becomes women of pious profession, through good works" (1 Timothy 2:8–10). Instructive, too, for prayer "as we ought" is the passage: "If then you are offering your gift at the altar and there think you that your brother has aught against you, leave there your gift before the altar, and go back—first be reconciled to your brother, and then come and offer your gift" (Matthew 5:23–24); for what greater gift can be sent up to God from a rational creature than fragrant words of prayer that is offered from a conscience devoid of taint from sin? Similarly instructive is: "Deprive not one another, save by agreement for a season that you may give yourselves to prayer and may be together at another time again, in order that Satan may not have occasion to exalt over you by reason of your incontinence" (1 Corinthians 7:5).

For prayer "as we ought" is restrained unless the marriage mysteries which claim our silence be consummated with more of solemnity and deliberation and less of passion, the "agreement" referred to in the passage obliterating the discord of passion, and destroying incontinence, and preventing Satan's malicious exultation. Yet again instructive for prayer "as we ought" is the passage, "If you are standing at prayer, forgive aught that you have against any man" (Mark 11:25); and also the passage in Paul "Any man who prays or preaches with covered head dishonors his head, and any woman who prays or preaches with unveiled head dishonors her head" (1 Corinthians 11:14–15) is descriptive of the right manner of prayer.

Paul knows all these sayings and could cite, with subtle statement in each case, manifold more from law and prophets and gospel fulfillment, but in the moderation, yes, and in the truthfulness of his nature, and because he sees how much, after all of them, is lacking to knowledge of the right way to pray what he ought, he says, "But what we ought to pray, we know not how to as we ought," and adds thereto the source from which a man's deficiency is made up if though ignorant he has rendered himself worthy to have the deficiency made up within him: "The Spirit himself more than intercedes with God in sighs unspeakable and he that searches hearts knows what is the mind of the Spirit, because his intercession on behalf of saints is according to God" (Romans 8:26–27). Thus the Spirit who cries "Abba, Father" (Romans 8:15) in the hearts of the blessed, knowing with solicitude that their sighing in this tabernacle can but weigh down the already fallen or transgressors, "more than intercedes with God in sighs unspeakable," for the great love and sympathy he feels for men taking our sighs upon himself; and, by virtue of the wisdom that resides in him, beholding our Soul humbled unto dust and shut within the body of humiliation, he employs no common sighs when he more than intercedes with God, but unspeakable ones akin to the unutterable words which a man may not speak. Not content to intercede with God, this Spirit intensifies his intercession, "more than intercedes," for those who more than conquer, as I believe such as Paul was, who says, "Nay in all these we more than conquer" (Romans 8:37).

He simply "intercedes," I think, not for those who more than conquer, nor again for those who are conquered, but for those who conquer. Akin to the saying, "What we ought to pray, we know not how to as we ought, but the Spirit more than intercedes with God in sighs unspeakable" is the passage "I will pray with the Spirit, and I will pray with the understanding also: I will sing with the spirit; and I will sing with the understanding also" (1 Corinthians 14:15).

For even our understanding is unable to pray unless the spirit leads it in prayer within hearing of it, as it were, anymore than it can sing or hymn, with rhythmic cadence and in unison, with true measure and in harmony, the Father in Christ, unless the Spirit who searches all things, even the depth of God, first praise and hymn him whose depth he has searched and, as he had the power, comprehended. I think it must have been the awakened consciousness of human weakness falling short of prayer in the right way, above all realized as he listened to great words of intimate knowledge falling from the Savior's lips in prayer to the Father, that moved one of the disciples of Jesus to say to the Lord when he ceased praying, "Lord, teach us to pray, even as John also taught his disciples" (Luke 11:1). The whole train of language is as follows: "And it came to pass, as he was at prayer in a certain place, that one of his disciples said to him when he ceased, 'Lord, teach us to pray even as John also taught his disciples.'"

For is it conceivable that a man who had been brought up under instruction in the law and hearing of the words of the prophets and was no stranger to the synagogue had no knowledge whatsoever of prayer until he saw the Lord praying in a certain place? It is absurd to pretend that he was one who did pray after the Jewish practice but saw that he needed fuller knowledge as to the place in reference to prayer. What was it, too, in reference to prayer that John used to teach the disciples who came to him for baptism from Jerusalem and all Judea and the country round about, but certain things of which, as one who was greater than a prophet, he had vision in reference to prayer, which I believe he would not deliver to all who were baptized but privately to those who were disciples with a view to baptism?

Such are the prayers which are really spiritual, because the spirit was praying in the heart of the saints, recorded in scripture, and they are full of unutterably wonderful declarations. In the first book of Samuel there is the prayer of Hannah, partially, because the whole of it was not committed to writing, since she was speaking in her heart (1 Samuel 1:13) when she perservered in prayer before the Lord; and in Psalms, the seventeenth psalm is entitled "A prayer of David," and the ninetieth "A prayer of Moses, man of God," and the hundred and second "A prayer of a poor man at a time he is weary and pours forth his supplication before the Lord."

These are prayers which, because truly prayers made and spoken with the spirit, are also full of the declarations of the wisdom of God, so that one may say of the truths they proclaim: "Who is wise that he shall understand them? And understanding, then he shall fully know them" (Hosea 14:9). Since therefore it is so great an undertaking to write about prayer, in order to think and speak worthily of so great a subject, we need the special illumination of the Father, and the teaching of the first-born Word himself, and the inward working of the Spirit, I pray as a man—for I by no means attribute to myself any capacity for prayer—that I may obtain the Spirit of prayer before I discourse upon it, and I entreat that a discourse full and spiritual may be granted to us and that the prayers recorded in the Gospels may be elucidated.

So let us now begin our discourse on Prayer.

CHAPTER 2

Scriptural uses of the general words for prayer

So far as I have observed, the first instance of the term "prayer" that I find is when Jacob, a fugitive from his brother Esau's wrath, was on his way to

Mesopotamia at the suggestion of Isaac and Rebecca. The passage runs: "And Jacob vowed a vow [prayed a prayer], saying—If the Lord God will be with me, and guard me in this way that I am going, and give me bread to eat and raiment to put on, and bring me back in safety to my father's house, then shall the Lord be my God and this stone which I have set up as a pillar shall be for me God's house, and of all that you will give me I will give you tithe" (Genesis 28:20–22).

It should also to be remarked that the term "prayer" is in many places is different from prayer as we speak of it—as when applied in the case of one who professes that he will do certain things in exchange for obtaining certain other things from God. The expression prayer is, however, employed in our usual sense [in early texts]. Thus in Exodus, after the scourge of frogs, the second in order of the ten, "Pharaoh called for Moses and Aaron and said to them: Pray unto the Lord for me that he withdraw the frogs from me and from my people; and I will send the people forth that they may sacrifice to the Lord" (Exodus 8:8).

And if, because Pharaoh's word is *aw-thar'* anyone should be skeptical as to *aw-thar'* meaning here prayer as well as vow, he should observe what follows: "Moses said to Pharaoh, 'Kindly tell me when I am to pray (*aw-thar'*) for you and for your officials and for your people, that the frogs may be removed from you and your houses and be left only in the Nile'" (Exodus 8:5). In the case of the fleas, the third scourge, I have observed that neither does Pharaoh entreat that prayer be made nor does Moses pray. In the case of the flies, the fourth, he says, "Pray therefore unto the Lord for me."

Then Moses also said: "I will go out from you and pray unto God, and the flies shall go away from Pharaoh and his servants and his people tomorrow" (Exodus 8:25). And shortly after: "So Moses went out from Pharaoh and prayed unto God." Again in the case of the fifth and the sixth scourge neither did Pharaoh entreat that prayer should be made nor did Moses pray, but in the case of the seventh Pharaoh sent and called for Moses and Aaron and said to them: "I have sinned this time; the Lord is righteous, I and my people are impious. Therefore pray unto the Lord that there be an end of thunder and hail and fire" (Exodus 9:27–28). And shortly after: "Moses went out from Pharaoh outside the city, and stretched forth his hands unto the Lord and there was an end to the thunder" (Exodus 9:33). Why is it not as in the foregoing cases?

And he prayed, but he stretched forth his hands unto the Lord. That is a question to be considered more conveniently elsewhere. In the case of the eighth scourge, however, Pharaoh says, "And pray (*aw-thar'*) to the Lord your God that at the least he remove this deadly thing from me." So Moses went out from Pharaoh and prayed (*aw-thar'*) unto God. We said that the term "prayer" (*aw-thar'*) is, as in Jacob's case, in many places employed in a sense other than the customary. In Leviticus for instance: "The Lord spoke to Moses saying, Speak to the children of Israel; and you shall say unto them: Whoever vows (*naw-dar'*) a vow (*neh'-der*), setting a price upon his soul to the Lord, his price, if a male from twenty to sixty years, shall be fifty didrachims of silver, sanctuary standard" (Leviticus 27:1–3). And in Numbers: "And the Lord spoke to Moses saying, Speak to the children of Israel; and you shall say unto them: Man or woman, whoever vows (*naw-dar'*) a great vow of consecration to the Lord, shall be consecrate from wine and strong drink"—and so on of the so-called Nazarite; then, shortly after—"and shall hallow his head in that day in which he was hallowed to the Lord for the days of the vow" (Numbers 6:1–3, 5).

And again shortly after: "This is the law for him that has vowed when he shall have fulfilled the days of his vow." And again shortly after: "And after that, he that has vowed will drink wine." This is the law for him that has vowed, whoever has vowed his votive gift to the Lord, apart from what his hand may find by virtue of his vow which he has vowed according to the law of consecration. And towards the end of Numbers: "And Moses spoke to the rulers of the tribes of the children of Israel saying, This is the thing which the Lord has decreed: A man who has vowed a vow to the Lord or sworn an oath or entered a bond, on his soul shall not desecrate his word: all that has gone out of his mouth shall he do" (Numbers 30:2–3).

And if a woman has vowed a vow to the Lord or entered a bond in the house of her father in her youth, and her father has heard her vows and her bonds that she entered into against her soul, and her father has let them pass in silence, all her vows shall stand, and her bonds that she entered into against her soul shall remain: after which he lays down sundry other laws for such a woman. In this sense it is written in Proverbs, "It is a snare to a man to hallow hastily anything of his own: for after vowing comes repenting" (Proverbs 20:25). And in Ecclesiastes: "Better not vow than vow without paying" (Ecclesiastes 5:5); and in the Acts of the Apostles: "There are among us four men of their own accord under a vow" (Acts 21:23).

I thought it not out of place first to distinguish the meaning of "prayer" (*aw-thar'*) in its two senses, and similarly of "prayer" (*neh'-der*), for the latter turn, in addition to its common and customary general usage, is also employed in the sense which we are accustomed to attach to vow, in what is told of Hannah in the first book of Samuel: "Now Eli the priest was sitting on a seat at the doorway of the temple of the Lord. And she was in bitterness of soul and prayed (*paw-lal'*) unto the Lord and wept sore. And she vowed (*naw-dar'*) a vow (*neh'-der*) and said: O Lord of hosts, if you will indeed look on the humiliation of your bondwoman and remember me and forget not your bondwoman and will give to your bondwoman male seed, then will I give him in gift to the Lord all the days of his life, and no razor shall come upon his head" (1 Samuel 1:9–11). And yet in this instance, one may, not without plausibility, with special regard to the words "she prayed (*paw-lal'*) unto the Lord," "and she vowed a vow," ask whether, as she has done both of two things, that is "prayed unto the Lord" "and vowed a vow," the word "prayed" (*paw-lal'*) on the one hand is not employed in our customary signification of prayer (*aw-thar'*), and "vowed a vow" on the other hand in the sense in which it is employed in Leviticus and Numbers. For, "I will give him in gift to the Lord all the days of his life, and no razor shall come upon his head" is strictly not a prayer but such a vow as Jephthah also vowed in the passage; and Jephthah vowed a vow to the Lord and said: "If you will indeed deliver the children of Ammon into my hand, then it shall be that whoever comes out of the doors of my house to meet me on my return in peace from the children of Ammon shall be the Lord's and I will offer him up as a burnt offering" (Judges 11:30–31).

CHAPTER 3

Objections to prayer

If then I must next, as you have urged, set forth in the first place the arguments of those who told that nothing is accomplished as a result of prayers and therefore allege that prayer is superfluous, I shall not hesitate to do that also according to my ability—the term "prayer" being now used in its more common and general sense. In such disrepute indeed is the view, and to such a degree has it failed to obtain champions of distinction, that among those who admit a Providence and set a God over the universe, not a soul can be found who does not believe in prayer.

The opinion (sentiment) belongs either to utter atheists who deny the existence of God, or assume a God, as far as the name goes, but deprive him of providence. Already, it must be said, the adverse inworking, with intent to wrap the most impious of opinions around the name of Christ and around the teaching of the Son of God, has made some converts on the needlessness of prayer—a sentiment which find champions in those who by every means do away with outward forms, eschewing Baptism and Eucharist alike, misrepresenting the Scriptures as not actually meaning this that we call prayer but as teaching something quite different from it.

Those who reject prayers, while, that is to say, setting a God over the universe and affirming Providence—for it is not my present task to consider the statements of those who by every means do away with a God or Providence—might reason as follows: God knows all things before they come to be. There is nothing that upon its entrance into existence is then first known by him as previously unknown. What need to send up prayer to One who, even before we pray, knows what things we have need of? For the heavenly Father knows what things we have need of before we ask him (Matthew 6:8).

It is reasonable to believe that as Father and Artificer of the universe, who loves all things that are and abhors nothing that he has made, quite apart from prayer he safely manages the affairs of each like a father who champions his infant children without awaiting their entreaty when they are either utterly incapable of asking or through ignorance often desirous of getting the opposite of what is to their profit and advantage. We men come further short of God even than the merest children of the intelligence of their parents. And in all likelihood the things that are to be are not only foreknown but prearranged by God, and nothing takes place contrary to his prearrangement. Were anyone to pray for sunrise he would be thought a simpleton for entreating through prayer for the occurrence of what was to take place quite apart from his prayer. In like manner a man would be a fool to believe that his prayer was responsible for the occurrence of what was to take place in any case even had he never prayed.

And again, as it is the height of madness to imagine that, because one suffers discomfort and fever under the sun at summer solstice, the sun is through prayer to be transferred to the springtime zodiac, in order that one may have the benefit of temperate air, so it would be the height of infatuation to imagine that by reason of prayer one would not experience the misfortunes that meet the race of men by necessity. Moreover, if it be true that sinners are estranged from birth, and the righteous man has been set apart from his mother's womb, and if, while as yet they are unborn and have done neither good nor evil, it is said the elder shall serve the younger, that the elective purpose of God may stand based not on works but on the Caller, it is in vain that we entreat for forgiveness of sins or to receive a spirit of strength to the end that, Christ empowering us, we may have strength for all things.

If we are sinners, we are estranged from birth: if on the other hand we were set apart from our mother's womb, the best of things will come our way even though we do not pray. It is prophesied before his birth

that Jacob shall be over Esau and that his brother shall serve him: what
has prayer to do with that? Of what impiety is Esau guilty that he is hated
before his birth? To what purpose does Moses pray, as is found in the
ninetieth psalm, if God is his refuge since before the mountains were
settled and the earth and world were formed. Besides, of all that are to
be saved, it is recorded in the Epistle to Ephesians that the Father elected
them in him, in Christ, before the world's foundation, that they should
be holy and blameless before him, preordaining them unto adoption as
his sons through Christ (Ephesians 1:4–5).

Either, therefore, a man is elect, of the number of those who are so
since before the world's foundation, and can by no means fall from his
election in which case he has therefore no need of prayer; or he is not
elect nor yet preordained, in which case he prays in vain, since, though
he should pray ten thousand times, he will not be listened to. For whom
God foreknew, them he also preordained to conformity with the image
of his Son's glory; and whom he preordained, them he also called; and
whom he called, them he also justified; and whom he justified, them he
also glorified (Romans 8:29–30).

Why is Josiah distressed, or why has he anxiety as to whether or not
he will be listened to in prayer, when, many generations before, he was
prophesied by name and his future action not only foreknown but fore-
told in the hearing of many? To what purpose, too, does Judas pray with
the result that even his prayer turned to sin, when from David's times
it is pre-announced that he will lose his overseership, another receiving
it in his stead?

It is self-evidently absurd, God being unchangeable and having
pre-comprehended all things and adhering to his prearrangements, to
pray in the belief that through prayer one will change his purpose, or,
as though he had not already prearranged but awaited each individual's
prayer, to make intercession that he may arrange what suits the supplicant
by reason of his prayer, there and then appointing what he approves as
reasonable though he has previously not contemplated it. At this point
the propositions you formulated in your letter to me may be set down

word for word thus: Firstly, if God is foreknower of the future and it must come to pass, prayer is vain. Secondly, if all things come to pass by virtue of God's will, and his decrees are fixed, and nothing that he wills can be changed, prayer is vain. Towards a solution of the difficulties which benumb the instinct of prayer, the following, as I believe, helpful considerations may be advanced.

CHAPTER 4

Answer to objections: Man's freewill and God's foreknowledge

Of objects that move, some have the cause of motion outside them. Such are objects which are lifeless and in passive motion simply by force of condition, and those which are moved by force of nature and of life in the same manner and not like things which move occasionally, for stones and stocks that have been quarried or cut off from growth, being in passive motion simply by force of condition, have the cause of motion outside them.

Such, too, are dead bodies of animals and movable parts of plants, which change position under compulsion and not as animals and plants themselves change their position but in the same manner as stones and stocks cut off from growth—although even these may be said to move in respect that, all bodies in decay being in flux, they possess the motion inherently attendant upon decay. Besides these, a second class of moving objects are those which move by force of their internal nature or life, which are said by those who use terms in their stricter sense to move of themselves.

A third kind of movement is that in animals, which is termed spontaneous movement, whereas, in my opinion, the movement of rational beings is independent movement. If we withdraw from an animal spontaneous movement, it cannot be any longer conceived as even an animal; it will be like either a plant moving by mere force of nature or a stone borne along by some force external to it. Whenever an object follows its own peculiar movement, since that is what we have termed "independent movement," it must needs be rational. Thinkers therefore who will have it that nothing is in our power will necessarily assent to a most foolish statement, firstly that we are not animals, and secondly that neither are we rational beings; but that, what we are believed to do, we may be said to do by force, as it were, of some external cause of motion and in no sense moving ourselves.

Let anyone, moreover, with special regard to his own feelings, see whether without shame he can deny that it is himself that wills, eats, walks, gives assent to and accepts certain opinions, dissents from others as false. There are certain opinions to which a man cannot possibly assent, though he puts them with innumerable refinements of argument and with plausible reasoning: and similarly it is impossible to assent to any view of human affairs in which our free will is in no sense preserved.

Who assents to the view that nothing is comprehensible, or lives as in complete suspense of judgement? Who that has received a sense perception of a domestic misdeed forebears to reprove the servant? And who is there that does not censure a son who fails to pay the duty owed to parents, or does not blame and find fault with an adulteress as having committed a shameful act? Truth forces and compels us, in spite of innumerable refinements, to impulsive praise and blame, on the basis of our retention of free will with the responsibility in which it involves us.

If our free will is in truth preserved with innumerable inclinations towards virtue or vice, towards either duty or its opposite, its future must like other things have been known by God, before coming to pass, from the world's creation and foundation; and in all things prearranged by God in accordance with what he has seen of each act of our free wills. He has with due regard to each movement of our free wills prearranged what also is at once to occur in his providence and to take place according to the train of future events. God's foreknowledge is not the cause of all future events, including those that are to have their efficient cause in our freewill guided by impulse.

Even though we should suppose God ignorant of the future, we shall not on that account be incapacitated for effecting this and willing that. Rather it ensues from his foreknowledge that our individual free wills receive adjustment to suit the universal arrangement needful for the constitution of the world. If, therefore, our individual free wills have been known by him, and if in his providence he has on that account been careful to make due arrangement for each one, it is reasonable to believe that he has also pre-comprehended what a particular man is to pray in that faith, what his disposition, and what his desire.

That being so, in his arrangement it will accordingly have been ordained somewhat after this wise: This man I will hear for the sake of the prayer that he will pray, because he will pray wisely: but that man I will not hear, either because he will be unworthy of being heard, or because his prayer will be for things neither profitable for the suppliant to receive nor becoming me to bestow: and in the case of this prayer, of some particular person, let us say, "I will not hear him," but in the case of that, "I will."

Should the fact of God's unerring foreknowledge of the future disquiet anyone by suggesting that things have been necessarily determined, we must tell him that it is a real part of God's fixed knowledge that a particular man will not with any fixed certainty choose the better or so desire the worse as to become incapable of a change for his good. And again: "I will do this for this man when he prays, as becomes me seeing that he will pray without reproach and will not be negligent in prayer: upon that man who will pray for a certain amount, I will bestow this abundantly in excess of his asking or thinking, for it becomes me to surpass him in well doing and to furnish more than he has been capable of asking.

"To this other man of a particular character I will send this angel as minister, to cooperate from a certain time in his salvation and to be with him for a certain period: to that other, who will be a better man than he, that angel of higher rank than his. From this man who, after having devoted himself to the higher views will gradually relax and fall back upon the more material, I will withdraw this superior cooperator, upon whose withdrawal that duly inferior power, having found an opportunity to get at his slackness, will set upon him and when he has given himself up in readiness to sin, will incite him to these particular sins."

So we may imagine the Prearranger of All saying: "Amos will beget Josiah, who will not emulate his father's faults but will find his way leading on to virtue, and will by aid of these companions be noble and good, so that he will tear down the evilly erected altar of Jeroboam. I also know that Judas, in the sojourn of my son among the race of men, will at the first be noble and good but later turn aside and fall away to human sins, so that he will rightly suffer thus for them." This foreknowledge, it may be in regard to all things, certainly in regard to Judas and other mysteries, exists in the Son of God also, who in his discernment of the evolution of the future has seen Judas and the sins to be committed by him, so that, even before Judas came into existence, he in his comprehension has said through David the words beginning, "O God, do not keep silence at my praise" (Psalm 83:1).

"Knowing as I do the future and what an influence Paul will have in the cause of religion, ere yet I set me to begin creation and found the world I will make choice of him: I will commit him from the moment of his birth to these powers that cooperate in men's salvation. I will set him apart from his mother's womb. I will permit him at the first to fall in youth into an ignorant zeal and in the avowed cause of religion to persecute believers in my Christ and to keep the garments of them that stone my servant and witness Stephen, so that later at the close of his youthful willfulness he may be given a fresh start and change for the best and yet not boast before me but may say, 'I am not fit to be called an apostle, because I persecuted the church of God' (1 Corinthians 15:9), and realizing the kindness that he will receive from me after his faults committed in youth in the avowed cause of religion may declare, 'It is by God's grace that I am what I am' (1 Corinthians 15:10); and, being restrained by conscience by reason of the deeds he wrought while still young against Christ, he will not be excessively elated by the exceeding abundance of the revelations which in kindness I shall show him."

To the objection in reference to prayer for the rising of the sun, we may reply as follows. The sun also possesses a certain free will, since he with the moon joins in praising God, for "Praise him, sun and moon" (Psalm 148:3), it says: as also manifestly the moon and all the stars conformably, for it says "Praise him all the stars and light." As, therefore, we have said that God has employed the free will of individual beings on earth for the service of beings on earth in arranging them aright, so we may suppose that he has employed the free will, fixed and certain and steadfast and wise as it is, of sun, moon, and stars in arranging the whole world of heaven with the course and movement of the stars in harmony with the whole.

If I do not pray in vain for what concerns any other freewill, much more shall I pray for what concerns the freewill of the stars which tread in heaven their world-conserving measures. It may indeed be said of beings on earth that certain appearances in our surroundings call out now our instability, now our better inclination, to act or speak in certain ways: but in the case of beings in heaven, what appearances can interpose to oust and remove from the course that benefit the world beings which have each a life so adjusted by Reason independently of them, and which enjoy so ethereal and supremely pure a frame?

CHAPTER 5
Answer to objections: Conditions necessary to prayer

With a view to impel men to pray and to turn them from neglect of prayer, we may not unreasonably further use an illustration such as this. Just as, apart from woman and apart from recourse to the function requisite for procreation, man cannot procreate, so one may not obtain certain things without prayer in a certain manner, with a certain disposition, with a certain faith, after a certain antecedent mode of life. Thus we are not to babble or ask for little things or pray for earthly things or enter upon prayer with anger and with thoughts disturbed.

Nor again is it possible to think of giving oneself to prayer apart from purification. Nor again is forgiveness of sins possible to the supplicant unless from the heart he forgives his brother who has done wrong and entreats him to obtain his pardon. That benefit accrues to him who prays rightly or according to his ability strives to do so, follows, I consider, in many ways. It is, first of all, surely in every sense a spiritual advantage to him who is intent upon prayer, in the very composure of prayer to present himself to God and in his presence to speak to him with a vivid sense that he looks on and is present. For just as certain mental images and particular recollections connected with the objects recollected may sully the thoughts suggested by certain other images, in the same way we may believe that it is advantageous to remember God as the object of our faith—the One who discerns the movements within the inner sanctuary of the soul as it disposes itself to please the Examiner of Hearts and Inquisitor of Reins as One who is present and beholds and penetrates into every mind.

Even though further benefit than this be supposed to accrue to him who has composed his thoughts for prayer, no ordinary gain is to be conceived as gotten by one who has devoutly disposed himself in the season of prayer. When this is regularly practiced, how many sins it keeps us from, and how many achievements it brings us to, is known only to those who have given themselves up with some degree of constancy to prayer.

For if the recollection and contemplation of a man who has found fame and benefit in wisdom incite us to evaluate him and sometimes restrains our lower impulses, how much more does the recollection of God, the Father of All, along with prayer to him, become advantageous to those who are persuaded that they stand before and speak to a present and hearing God!

What I have said may be established from the divine scriptures in the following way. He who prays must lift up holy hands, forgiving everyone who has wronged him, with the passion of anger banished from his soul and in wrath with none. And again, to prevent his mind from being made turbid by irrelevant thoughts, he must while at prayer forget for the time everything outside prayer—surely a state of supreme blessedness! As Paul

teaches in the first Epistle to Timothy when he says: "I desire therefore
that men pray in every place, lifting up holy hands without anger and
disputations" (1 Timothy 2:8). And further, a woman ought, most of all
at prayer, to preserve simplicity and decency in soul and body, above all
and especially while she prays reverencing God and expelling from her
intellect every wanton womanish recollection, arrayed not in chaplets
and gold or pearls or costly raiment, but in the things in which it becomes
a woman of pious profession to be arrayed. And I marvel that anyone
should hesitate, were it on the strength of such a condition alone, to
pronounce her blessed who has thus presented herself for prayer, as Paul
has taught in the same Epistle when he says, "In like manner that women
array themselves decently in simplicity with modesty and discretion, not
in chaplets and gold or pearls or costly raiment, but, as becomes woman
of pious profession, through good works" (1 Timothy 2:9–10).

And besides, the prophet David speaks of much else that the saint
possesses in prayer. We may, not irreverently, cite these passages as showing that, even if this alone be considered, the attitude and preparation for
prayer of one who has offered himself to God is of the highest benefit.
He says, "Unto you have I lifted my eyes, who dwells in heaven, and unto
you have I lifted my soul, O God" (Psalm 123:1; 25:1). For when the
eyes of thought are lifted up from dwelling on earthly things and being
filled with the imagination of material objects, and are elevated to such
a height as to look beyond begotten things and to be engaged solely in
contemplation of God and in solemn converse with him becoming to
the Hearer.

Surely those eyes themselves have already got the highest advantage in
reflecting the glory of the Lord with face unveiled and being transformed
into the same image from glory to glory, for they then partake of a certain
divine perception shown by the words, "The light of your face, O Lord,
has been signalized upon us" (Psalm 4:7). And indeed the soul being
lifted up, and parting from body to follow spirit, and not only following
the spirit but also merging in it, as is shown by the words "Unto you have
I lifted my soul," is surely already putting off its existence as soul and

becoming spiritual. And if forgiveness is a very high accomplishment—so high as according to the prophet Jeremiah to embrace a summary of the whole law, for he says, "I laid not those commands upon your fathers as they were gone forth from Egypt, but this command I laid: Let each man not be unforgiving to his neighbor in his heart"—and if in entering upon prayer with unforgiveness left behind us we keep the Savior's command, "If you are standing at prayer, forgive aught that you have against any man" (Mark11:25), it is plain that those who stand in that temper to pray have already received the best of possessions.

CHAPTER 6

Answer to objections: He who prays, prays not alone

So far, I have said that, even on the supposition that nothing else is going to follow our prayer, we receive the best of gains when we have come to perceive the right way to pray and when we achieve it. But it is certain that he who thus prays, having previously cast aside all discontent with Providence, will, if intent to mark the inworking of the Hearer, in the very act hear the response, "Here am I."

The above condition is expressed in the words, "If you withdraw your bonds and protests and murmuring utterance," for he that is content with what comes to pass becomes free from every bond, does not protest against God for ordaining what he wills for our discipline, and does not even in the secrecy of his thoughts murmur inaudibly; for they who murmur thus, not daring to abuse Providence roundly for what occurs with voice and soul, but desiring as it were to escape the observation even of the Lord of All in their discontent, are like bad domestics who rail, but not openly, against their masters' orders.

And I think the same thing is meant in the passage in Job, "In all these occurrences Job sinned not with his lips in the sight of God" (Job 2:10); and it is just this that the saying in Deuteronomy enjoins must not happen, when it says, "Take heed lest a secret utterance be ever in your heart to break the law, saying the seventh year draws nigh" (Deuteronomy 15:9), and so on. So then he who prays thus, becomes, as already so greatly benefited, more fit to mingle with the Spirit of the Lord that fills the whole world and fills all the earth and the heaven and says by the prophet, "'Do not I fill the heaven and the earth?' says the Lord" (Jeremiah 23:24).

And further, through the aforementioned purification as well as through prayer, he will enjoy the good office of the Word of God, who is standing in the midst even of those who do not know him and who fails the prayer of none, to pray to the Father along with him for whom he mediates. For the Son of God is high priest of our offerings and our pleader with the Father. He prays for those who pray, and pleads along with those who plead. He will not, however, consent to pray, as for his intimates, on behalf of those who do not with some constancy pray through him, nor will he be Pleader with the Father, as for men already his own, on behalf of those who do not obey his teaching to the effect that they ought at all times to pray and not lose heart (Luke 18:1).

For it says, "He spoke a parable to the end that they ought at all times to pray and not lose heart. There was a certain judge in a certain city" (Luke 18:1–2), and so on; and earlier he said unto them, "Who of you shall have a friend, and shall go unto him at midnight and shall say to him: Friend, lend me three loaves, since a friend of mine has come to me after a journey and I have naught to set before him" (Luke 11:5); and a little later, "I tell you, even though he will not rise and give him because he is his friend, he will yet because of his being unabashed get up and give him as many as he wants" (Luke 11:8). And who that believes the guileless lips of Jesus can but be stirred to unhesitating prayer when he says, "Ask and it shall be given you . . . for everyone that asks receives" (Luke 11:9–10), since the kind Father gives to those who have received the spirit of adoption from the Father, the living bread when we ask him, not the stone which the adversary would have become food for Jesus and his disciples, and since The Father gives the good gift in rain from heaven to those that ask him.

But these pray along with those who genuinely pray—not only the high priest but also the angels who "rejoice in heaven over one repenting sinner more than over ninety-nine righteous that need not repentance" (Luke 15:7), and also the souls of the saints already at rest. Two instances make this plain. The first is where Raphael offers their service to God for Tobit and Sarah. After both had prayed, the scripture says, "The prayer of both was heard before the presence of the great Raphael, and he was sent to heal them both" (Tobit 3:16–17), and Raphael himself, when explaining his angelic commission at God's command to help them, says: "Even now when you prayed, and Sarah your daughter-in-law, I brought the memorial of your prayer before the Holy One" (Tobit 12:12), and shortly after, "I am Raphael, one of the Seven angels who present the prayers of saints and enter in before the glory of the Holy One" (Tobit 12:15). Thus, according to Raphael's account at least, prayer with fasting and almsgiving and righteousness is a good thing.

The second instance is in the Books of the Maccabees where Jeremiah appears in exceeding "white haired glory" so that a wondrous and most majestic authority was about him, and stretches forth his right hand and delivers to Judas a golden sword, and there witnesses to him another saint already at rest saying, "This is he who prays much for the people and the sacred city, God's prophet Jeremiah" (2 Maccabees 15:14). For it is absurd when knowledge, though manifested to the worthy through a mirror and in a riddle for the present, is then revealed face to face not to think that the like is true of all other excellences as well, that they who prepare in this life beforehand are made strictly perfect then.

Now one of these excellences in the strictest sense according to the divine word is love for one's neighbor, and this accordingly we are compelled to think of as possessed in a far higher degree by saints already at rest than by those who are in human weakness and wrestle on along with the weaker. It is not only here that "if one member suffers, all the members suffer with it, and if one member is glorified, all the members rejoice with it" (1 Corinthians 12:26) in the experience of those who love their brethren, for it beseems the love also of those who are beyond the present life to say, "I have anxiety for all the churches: Who is weak and I am not weak? Who is made to stumble and I do not burn?" Especially when Christ avows that according as such one of the saints may be weak, he is weak in like manner, and in prison and naked and a stranger and hungry and athirst. For who that reads the gospel is ignorant that Christ, in taking on himself whatever befalls believers, counts their sufferings his own?

And if angels of God came to Jesus and ministered to him, and if we are not to think of the ministry of the angels to Jesus as having been limited to the brief space of his bodily sojourn among men while he was still in the midst of believers, not as one that reclined at table but as one that ministered, how many angels, I wonder, must now be ministering to Jesus when he would "bring together the children of Israel one by one" (Isaiah 27:12) and gather them from the dispersion, saving those who fear God and call upon him, and must be cooperating more than the apostles in the increase and enlargement of the church! Thus in John certain angels are spoken of in the Apocalypse as actually presiding over the churches.

Not in vain do angels of God ascend and descend unto the Son of Man, beheld of eyes that have been enlightened with the light of knowledge. In the very season of prayer, accordingly, being reminded by the suppliant of his needs, they satisfy them as they have ability by virtue of their general commission. To further the acceptance of our view we may make use of some such image as the following in support of this argument.

Suppose that a righteously minded physician is at the side of a sick man praying for health, with knowledge of the right mode of treatment for the disease about which the man is offering prayer. It is manifest that he will be moved to heal the suppliant, surmising, it may well be not idly, that God has had this very action in mind in answer to the prayer of the suppliant for release from the disease. Or suppose that a man of considerable means, who is generous, hears the prayer of a poor man offering intercession to God for his wants. It is plain that he, too, will fulfill the objects of the poor man's prayer, becoming a minister of the fatherly counsel of him who at the season of the prayer had brought together him who was to pray and him who was able to supply and by virtue of the rightness of his principles, incapable of overlooking one who has made that particular request.

As therefore we are not to believe that these events are fortuitous, when they take place because he who has numbered all the hairs of the head of saints, has aptly brought together at the season of the prayer the hearer who is to be minister of his benefaction to the suppliant and the man who has made his request in faith; so we may surmise that the presence of the angels who exercise oversight and ministry for God is sometimes brought into conjunction with a particular suppliant in order that they may join in breathing his petitions.

Nay more, beholding ever the face of the Father in heaven and looking on the Godhead of our Creator, the angel of each man, even of "little ones" within the church, both prays with us, and acts with us where possible, for the objects of our prayer.

CHAPTER 7

Answer to objections: The true place of prayer in man's life

Again I believe the words of the prayer of the saints to be full of power above all when praying "with the spirit," they pray "also with the understanding" (1 Corinthians 14:15), which is like a light rising from the suppliant's mind and proceeding from his lips to gradually weaken by the power of God the mental venom injected by the adverse powers into the intellect of such as neglect prayer and fail to keep that saying of Paul's in accordance with the exhortations of Jesus, "Pray without ceasing" (1 Thessalonians 5:17). For it is as if a dart from the suppliant's soul, sped by knowledge and reason or by faith, proceeds from the saint and wounds to their destruction and dissolution the spirits adverse to God and desirous of casting round us the bonds of sin.

Now, since the performance of actions enjoined by virtue or by the commandments is also a constituent part of prayer, he prays without ceasing who combines prayer with right actions, and becoming actions with prayer. For the saying "pray without ceasing" can only be accepted by us as a possibility if we may speak of the whole life of a saint as one great continuous prayer.

Of such prayer, what is usually termed prayer is indeed a part, and ought to be performed at least three times each day, as is plain from the account of Daniel who, in spite of the grave danger that impended, prayed three times daily. Peter furnishes an instance of the middle prayer of the three when he goes up to the housetop about the sixth hour to pray on that occasion on which he also saw the vessel which descended from heaven let down by four corners. The first is spoken of by David: "In the morning shall you hear my prayer: in the morning will I present myself to you and keep watch" (Psalm 5:3).

The last is indicated in the words, "the lifting up of my hands in evening sacrifice" (Psalm 141:2). Indeed we shall not rightly speak even the season of night without such prayer as David refers to when he says "at midnight I arose to make acknowledgment to you for your righteous judgments" (Psalm 119:62) and as Paul exemplifies when, as it is said in the Acts of the Apostles, along with Silas he offers prayer and praise to God "about midnight" (Acts 16:25) in Phillipi so that the prisoners also heard them.

CHAPTER 8
Answer to objections: Signal instances of prayer

If Jesus prays and does not pray in vain, if he obtains his requests through prayer and it may be would not have received them without prayer, who of us is to neglect prayer? Mark tells us that "in the morning, long before daybreak, he arose and went out and departed to a lonely place and there prayed" (Mark 1:35). Luke says: "And it came to pass, as he was at prayer in a certain place, that one of his disciples said to him when he ceased"

(Luke 11:1), and elsewhere, "And he passed the night in prayer to God" (Luke 6:12). John records a prayer of him in the words: "These things spoke Jesus, and lifting up his eyes unto heaven he said, Father the hour is come; glorify your Son that your Son may also glorify you" (John 17:1). And the Lord's saying, "I knew that you hear me always" (John 11:42), recorded in the same writer, shows that it is because he is always praying that he is always heard.

What need is there to tell the tale of those who, through right prayer, have obtained the greatest of things from God, when it is open to everyone to select any number of them for himself from the Scriptures? Hannah did service to the birth of Samuel, who is numbered along with Moses, because though barren she prayed in faith unto the Lord. Hezekiah, who while still childless learned from Isaiah that he was about to die, is included in the Savior's genealogy because he prayed. When the people were already on the point of perishing under a single decree as the result of Haman's conspiracy, it was the heard prayer with fasting of Mordecai and Esther that added to the Mosaic festivals and gave rise to the Mordecaic day of rejoicing for the people.

It was, moreover, after offering holy prayer that Judith with God's help overcame Holophernes, and thus a single woman of the Hebrews wrought shame upon the house of Nebuchadnezzar. It was on being heard that Ananiah and Azariah and Mishael became worthy to receive a hissing rain and wind which kept the flame of the fire from taking effect. Through Daniel's prayers, the lions in the Babylonians' pit were muzzled.

Even Jonah, because he did not despair of being heard from the belly of the monster that had swallowed him, was able to quit the monster's belly and complete his interrupted prophet's mission to the Ninevites. And further, how many things could each of us recount should he choose to recall with gratitude the benefits conferred upon him and to offer praise to God for them! Souls that have long been barren but have become conscious of their intellects' sterility and the barrenness of their mind, through persevering prayer have conceived of the Holy Spirit and given birth to thoughts and words of salvation full of contemplated truth.

How many of our foes have been dispersed, when often countless thousands in the adverse host were wearing us down with intent to sweep us away from the divine faith, and we rejoiced, when their appeal was to chariots and horses but ours to the name of the Lord, to see that in truth deceptive is a horse for safety! Many a time indeed does he whose trust is in praise to God—for "Judith" means praise—cut his way through guileful and persuasive speech, that chief commander of the adversary who brings numbers even of reputed believers to their knees.

What need is there to go on to tell of all who many a time have fallen among temptations hard to overcome, whose burn was sharper than any flame, and have suffered naught under them, but emerged from them in every way unscathed, without so much of scathe as the slightest odor of the hostile fire; or again of all the brutes exasperated against us, in the form of wicked spirits or cruel men, that we have encountered and often muzzled by our prayers, so that they were impotent to fasten their fangs in our members which had become those of Christ. Often in each saint's experience has the Lord dashed together the teeth of lions, and they were brought to nothing, as water flowing by.

We know that often fugitives from God's commands who have been swallowed by death, which at the first prevailed against them, have been saved by reason of repentance from so great an evil, because they did not despair of being able to be saved though already overpowered in the belly of death: for death prevailed and swallowed, and again God took away every tear from every face. What I have said after my enumeration of persons who have been benefited through prayer, I consider to have been most necessary to my purpose of turning aspirants after the spiritual life in Christ from prayer for little earthly things, and urging readers of this writing towards the mystical things of which the above mentioned were types.

For it is always and wholly prayer for the spiritual, mystical things which we have instanced, that is practiced by him who does not war according to the flesh but with the Spirit mortifies the body's actions, preference being given to the things suggested by analogy and study over the benefaction apparently indicated by the language of scripture as having accrued to those who had prayed.

For in ourselves also we are to strive, hearing the spiritual law with spiritual ears, that barrenness or sterility may not arise, but that we may like Hannah and Hezekiah be heard, being freed from barrenness or sterility, and like Mordecai and Esther and Judith be delivered from plotting enemies—in our case the spiritual powers of evil. Inasmuch as Egypt is an iron furnace and also a symbol of every earthly place, let everyone who has escaped from the wickedness of the life of men without having been scorched by sin or having had his heart like an oven full of fire, give thanks no less than the men who experienced rain amid fire.

Let him, too, who has been heard when he has prayed and said, "Deliver not to the brutes a soul that makes acknowledgment to you," and who has suffered naught from asp and basilisk because through Christ he has trod on them, and who has trampled lion and snake and enjoyed the good authority bestowed by Jesus to walk over serpents and scorpions and upon the whole power of the enemy, without having been injured by any of them, give thanks more than Daniel as having been delivered from brutes more terrible and harmful.

Let him, moreover, who has learned by experience what manner of monster that which swallowed Jonah typified, perceiving that it is of such that Job has spoken, "May he curse it that curses that day, he that is to worst the great monster," if he should ever come by reason of any disobedience to be in the belly of the monster, pray in penitence, and he shall come out thence; and if, after coming out, he abides in obedience to the commands of God, he shall be able according to the kindness of the Spirit to be a prophet to perishing Ninevites of today and to become a means to their salvation, without discontent with the kindness of God or desire that he should abide in severity towards penitents.

The very highest thing that Samuel is said to have done through prayer is spiritually possible of achievement today by every genuine dependant upon God who has become worthy to be heard. It is written: "And now do but stand and see this great thing which the Lord does under you eyes. Is it not wheat harvest today? I will call upon the Lord and he will give thunders and rain" (1 Samuel 12:16–17). And then shortly after it says, "And Samuel called upon the Lord, and the Lord gave thunders and rain in that day" (1 Samuel 12:18). To every saint who is genuinely in discipleship to Jesus it is said by the Lord, "Lift up your eyes and behold how the fields are white already unto harvest. He that harvests receives wages and gathers fruit unto life eternal" (John 4:35–36).

In this time of harvest the Lord does a great thing under the eyes of those who hear the prophets; for when he that is adorned by the Spirit calls upon the Lord, God gives from heaven thunders and rain that waters the Soul, in order that he who was before in vice may deeply fear the Lord and the minister of God's benefaction whose claim to reverence and veneration has been attested through the hearing of his prayers. Elijah indeed by a divine word opened the heavens after they had been shut to the impious three years and six months, a thing which anyone may accomplish at any time when through prayer he receives the Soul's rain, if he be one who has hitherto been deprived of it because of sin.

CHAPTER 9
The content of prayer: Its four moods

After thus interpreting the benefactions which have accrued to saints through their prayers, let us turn our attention to the words "Ask for the great things and the little shall be added unto you: and ask for the heavenly things and the earthly shall be added unto you" (Matthew 6:33). All symbolical and typical things may be described as little and earthly in comparison with the true and the spiritual.

And, I believe, the divine Word, in urging us on to imitate the prayers of the saints, speaks of the heavenly and great things set forth through those concerned with the earthly and little, in order that we may make our requests according to the reality of which their achievements were typical. He says in effect: You who would be spiritual, ask for the heavenly and great, in order that obtaining in them heavenly things you may inherit a kingdom of heaven, and as obtaining great things you may enjoy the greatest blessings, while as for the earthly and little that you require by reason of your bodily necessities, your Father will supply them to you in due measure.

In the first Epistle to Timothy, the Apostle has employed four terms corresponding to four things in close relation to the subject of devotion and prayer. It will therefore be of service to cite his language and see whether we can satisfactorily determine the strict meaning of each of the four. He says, "I exhort therefore first of all that requests, prayers, intercessions, thanksgivings be made on behalf of all men," and so on (1 Timothy 2).

"Request" I take to be that form of prayer which a man in some need offers with supplication for its attainment; "prayer," that which a man offers in the loftier sense for higher things with ascription of glory; "intercession," the addressing of claim to God by a man who possesses a certain fuller confidence; "thanksgiving," the prayerful acknowledgment of the attainment of blessings from God, he who returns the acknowledgment being impressed by the greatness, or what seems to the recipient the greatness, of the benefactions conferred. Of the first, examples are found in Gabriel's speech to Zechariah who, it is likely, had prayed for the birth of John: "Fear not, Zechariah, because your request has been heard, and your wife Elizabeth shall beget you a Son and you shall call his name John" (Luke 1:13); in the account in Exodus of the making of the calf: "And Moses made request before the Lord God, and said: To what purpose, Lord, are you in anger wroth with your people whom you have brought out of the land of Egypt in great might?" (Exodus 32:11).

In Deuteronomy: "And I made request before the Lord a second time even as also the former time forty days and forty nights bread I ate not and water I drank not for all your sins that you sinned" (Deuteronomy 9:18); and in Esther: "Mordecai made request of God, recalling all the works of the Lord, and said: Lord, Lord, King Almighty," and Esther herself "made request of the Lord God of Israel and said, Lord our King."

Of the second, examples are found in Daniel: "And Azariah drew himself up and prayed thus, and opening his mouth amid the fire said" (Daniel 3:25); and in Tobit: "And with anguish I prayed saying, Righteous are you, O Lord, and all your works; all your ways are mercy and truth, and judgment true and righteous do you judge forever" (Tobit 3:1–2). Since however, the circumcised have marked the passage in Daniel spurious, as not standing in the Hebrew, and dispute the Book of Tobit as not within the Testament, I shall cite Hannah's case from the first book of Samuel.

"And she prayed unto the Lord, and wept exceedingly, and vowed a vow, and said, O Lord of Hosts, if you will indeed have regard unto the humiliation of your bondmaid" (1 Samuel 1:11), and so on; and in Habakkuk: "A prayer of Habakkuk the prophet, set to song. O Lord, I have hearkened to your voice and was afraid; I did mark your works and was in ecstasy. In the midst of two living beings you shall be known; as the years draw nigh you shall be fully known" (Habakkuk 3:1–2); a prayer which eminently illustrates what I said in defining prayer that it is offered with ascription of glory by the suppliant. And in Jonah also, Jonah prayed unto the Lord his God from the belly of the monster, and said, "I cried in my affliction unto the Lord my God, and he heard me. You heard my wail from the belly of death, my cry; you flung me away into the depths of the heart of the sea, and streams encircled me" (Jonah 2:2–3).

Of the third, we have an example in the Apostle where he with good reason employs prayer in our case, but intercession in that of the Spirit as excelling us and having confidence in approaching him with whom he intercedes; for as to what we are to pray, he says, "as we ought we know not, but the Spirit himself more than intercedes with God in sighs unspeakable, and he that searches hearts knows what is the mind of the Spirit because his intercession on behalf of saints is according to God" (Romans 8:26); for the Spirit more than intercedes, and intercedes, whereas we pray.

What Joshua said concerning the sun's making a stand over against Gabaoth is, I think, also intercession: "Then spake Joshua to the Lord in the day when the Lord delivered up the Amorites before the children of Israel, and he said in the sight of Israel, Sun, stand still upon Gibeon; and you, Moon, in the valley of Ajalon" (Joshua 10:12); and in Judges, it is, I think, in intercession that Samson said, "Let my soul die together with the aliens" (Judges 16:30) when he leaned in might and the house fell upon the princes and upon all the people in it. Even though it is not explicitly said that Joshua and Samson interceded but that they said, their language seems to be intercession, which, if we accept the terms in their strict sense, is in our opinion distinct from prayer.

Of thanksgiving an example is our Lord's utterance when he says: "I make acknowledgment to you, O Father, Lord of heaven and earth, that you did hide these things from the wise and understanding and reveal them to infants" (Matthew 11:25); for "I make acknowledgment" is equivalent to "I give thanks."

CHAPTER 10

The recipient of prayer in its four moods

Now request and intercession and thanksgiving, it is not out of place to offer even to men—the two latter, intercession and thanksgiving, not only to saintly men but also to others. But request to saints alone, should some Paul or Peter appear, to benefit us by making us worthy to obtain the authority which has been given to them to forgive sins—with this addition indeed that, even should a man not be a saint and we have wronged him, we are permitted, our becoming conscious of our sin against him, to make request even of such, that he extend pardon to us who have wronged him.

Yet if we are offer thanksgiving to men who are saints, how much more should we give thanks to Christ, who has under the Father's will conferred so many benefactions upon us? Yes, and intercede with him as did Stephen when he said, "Lord, set not this sin against them" (Acts 7:60). In imitation of the father of the lunatic we shall say, "I request, Lord, have mercy," either on my son, or myself, or as the case may be. But if we accept prayer in its full meaning, we may not ever pray to any begotten being, not even to Christ himself, but only to the God and Father of All, to whom our Savior both prayed himself, as we have already instanced, and teaches us to pray.

For when he has heard one say, "Teach you us to pray," he does not teach men to pray to himself but to the Father saying, "Our Father in heaven," and so on (Luke 11:2-4; Matthew 6:9-13). For if, as is shown elsewhere, the Son is other than the Father in being and essence, prayer is to be made either to the Son and not the Father or to both or to the Father alone.

That prayer to the Son and not the Father is most out of place and only to be suggested in defiance of manifest truth, one and all will admit. In prayer to both, it is plain that we should have to offer our claims in plural form, and in our prayers say, "Grant you both," "Bless you both," "Supply you both," "Save you both," or the like, which is self-evidently wrong and also incapable of being shown by anyone to stand in the scriptures as spoken by any.

It remains, accordingly, to pray to God alone, the Father of All, not however apart from the High Priest who has been appointed by the Father with swearing of an oath, according to the words he has sworn and shall not repent, "You are a priest forever after the order of Melchizedek" (Psalm 110:4). In thanksgiving to God, therefore, during their prayers, saints acknowledge his favors through Christ Jesus.

Just as the man who is scrupulous about prayer ought not to pray to one who himself prays, but to the Father upon whom our Lord Jesus has taught us to call in our prayers, so we are not to offer any prayer to the Father apart from him. He clearly sets this forth himself when he says, "Verily, verily, I tell you, whatsoever you may ask of my Father, he shall give you in my house. Until but now, you have not asked aught in my name. Ask and you shall receive, that your joy may be fulfilled" (John 16:23-24).

He did not say, "Ask of me," nor yet simply "Ask of the Father," but "Whatsoever you may ask of the Father, he will give you in my name."

For until Jesus taught this, no one had asked of the Father in the name of the Son. True was the saying of Jesus, "Until but now you have not asked aught in my name"; and true also the words, "Ask and you shall receive, that your joy may be fulfilled." Should anyone, however who believes that prayer ought to be made to Christ himself, confused by the sense of the expression make obeisance, confront us with that acknowledged reference to Christ in Deuteronomy, "Let all God's angels make obeisance to him" (Deuteronomy 32:43), we may reply to him that the church, called Jerusalem by the prophet, is also said to have obeisance made to her by kings and queens who become her foster sires and nurses, in the words, "Behold, I lift up my hand upon the nations, and upon the isles will I lift up my sign: and they shall bring your sons in their bosom, and your daughters they shall lift up on their shoulders; and kings shall be your foster sires, their queens, their nurses: to the face of the earth shall they make obeisance to you, and the dust of your feet shall they lick: and you shall know that I am the Lord and shall not be ashamed" (Isaiah 49:22–23).

And how does it not accord with him who said: "Why do you call me good? None is good save One—God the Father" (Luke 18:19) to suppose that he would say, "Why do you pray to me? To the Father alone ought you to pray, to whom I also pray, as indeed you learn from the holy Scriptures. For you ought not to pray to one who has been appointed high priest for you by the Father and has received it from the Father to be advocate, but through a high priest and advocate able to sympathize with your weaknesses, having been tried in all points like you but, by reason of the Father's free gift to me, tried without sin. Learn you therefore how great a free gift you have received from my Father in having received through regeneration in me the Spirit of adoption, that you may be called sons of God and my brethren. For you have read my utterance spoken through David to the Father concerning you, 'I will proclaim your name to my brethren; in the midst of the church will I sing hymns to you' (Hebrews 2:12). It is not reasonable that those who have been counted worthy of one common Father should pray to a brother. To the Father alone you ought, with me and through me, to send up prayer."

So, then, hearing Jesus speak to such effect, let us pray to God through him, all with one accord and without division concerning the manner of prayer. Are we not indeed divided if we pray some to the Father, others to the Son—those who pray to the Son, whether with the Father or without the Father, committing a crude error in all simplicity for lack of discrimination and examination?

Let us therefore pray as to God, intercede as with a Father, request as of a Lord, give thanks as to God and Father and Lord, though in no way as to a servant's lord; for the Father may reasonably be considered Lord not only of the Son but also of those who through him are become sons also, though, just as he is not God of dead but of living men, so he is not Lord of baseborn servants but of such as at the first are ennobled by means of fear because they are as infants, but serve thereafter according to love in a service more blessed than that which is in fear. For within the soul itself, visible to the Seer of Hearts alone, these are distinctive characters of servants and sons of God.

CHAPTER 11
The objects of prayer

Everyone who asks for the earthly and little things from God disregards him who has enjoined the asking of heavenly and great things. God is incapable of bestowing anything either earthly or little. Should anyone suggest instances to the contrary in which the material things bestowed upon the saints in the past as a result of prayer, and indeed the express language of the Gospel when it teaches that the earthly and the little are to be added unto us, we may reply to him as follows.

When someone bestows upon us a particular material object, we should not say that the person has bestowed upon us the shadow of the object, for it is unintentional to present two things, object and shadow. The giver's intention is to give a material object; our receipt of its shadow is a consequence of the gift. In like manner if, with mind grown nobler, we have discerned the gifts that are principally given to us by God, we shall most properly describe as consequences of the great and heavenly spiritual gifts of grace the material things which are given to each of the saints for his good or in proportion to his faith or according as the Giver wills, and wisely does he will, even though we are unable to describe a cause and reason worthy of the Giver for each of his gifts.

Greater fruit had been borne by Hannah's soul in being turned from sterility than was her body in conceiving Samuel. Diviner had been the offspring begotten by Hezekiah's mind than that which was begotten of the material seed of his body. Higher had been the deliverances of Esther and Morecai and the people from spiritual plots than was that from Haman and his conspirators. Mightier was the prince that sought to ruin her soul, whose power Judith had cut through than he whom she met in Holophermes.

Who would not acknowledge that in the spiritual blessing which comes home to all the saints and which Isaac spoke of to Jacob, "God give you of the rain of heaven" (Genesis 27:28), a higher rain had fallen to Ananiah and those with him than the material rain that overcame Nebuchadnezzar's flame? Greater had been the muzzling of the unseen lions by the prophet Daniel, so that they were unable to work anything against his soul, than that of the visible lions to which all of us who read the passage have understood it to refer.

And who as a saint, becoming a fit recipient of the holy spirit, had ever, like Jonah, escaped the belly of a monster that swallowed every fugitive from God and which has been defeated by Jesus our Savior? It need not cause surprise if, to keep the metaphor, the corresponding shadow is not given to all who receive objects capable of making shadows, while to some a shadow is what is given. Students of questions relating to sundials and of the relation of shadows to the illuminating body clearly observe what is the case with bodies generally, that at a particular time some projectors are shadowless, others are short shadowed, others are more or less long-shadowed.

It is therefore not astonishing that, as the Giver's plan is to bestow the principal things in accordance with certain unutterable and mystic guiding principles and suitable to the recipients and occasions, when the principal objects are being given there should sometimes go with them no shadows at all for the recipients. At other times shadows are but few; at other times shadows which are smaller in comparison accompany different objects.

As the presence or absence of the shadow of bodies neither pleases nor pains the man whose object of search is solar beams, he possesses his chief necessity in being illumined or freed from shadow or in having more or less of shadow as the case may be. If the spiritual things are ours, and we are being illumined by God for complete possession of true blessings, we shall not quibble over a matter so paltry as concerns the shadow.

For material and physical things count as fleeting feeble shadow, in no way comparable to the saving holy gifts of the God of All. What comparison is there between material riches and the riches that are in every word and all wisdom? Who in his senses would compare health of flesh and bone with health of mind, strength of soul, and consistency of thought—things which, if kept in measure by God's word, make bodily sufferings a paltry scratch, and even slighter if we can grasp it?

He that has discerned the meaning of the beauty of the bride whom the bridegroom Word of God loves, a soul blooming with more than heavenly and more than mundane beauty, will be ashamed to dignify with the same name of beauty the physical beauty of woman or child or man. For of beauty in the strict sense flesh is not capable, being deformity throughout. For all flesh is as grass, and the glory thereof, which is manifest in the so called beauty of women and children, is according to the prophet's language compared to a flower: "All people are grass, their constancy is like the flower of the field. The grass withers, the flower fades, when the breath of the Lord blows upon it; surely the people are grass. The grass withers, the flower fades; but the word of our God will stand forever" (1 Peter 1:24–25).

Again, who that has perceived the nobility of the sons of God shall any longer give the name of nobility to what passes as such among men? After contemplating Christ's kingship over kings, how shall the mind not dispel all kingship upon earth? When the human mind, so far as capable while still bound to a body, has once beheld as clearly as may be an army of angels, and among them chief-commanders of the Lord's hosts, and archangels and thrones and lordships and principalities and more than heavenly authorities, and has come to understand that it can obtain from the Father their equivalent, how shall it not despise those things which, though frailer than shadow, are the admiration of the foolish, even if they should all be given to it, as most shadowy and in comparison insignificant, and look beyond in order not to fall short of obtaining the true principalities and diviner authorities?

We should therefore pray for the principal and truly great and heavenly things, and as for those concerned with the shadows accompanying the principal, commit them to the God who knows before we ask him what things, by reason if our perishable body, we have need.

CHAPTER 12

The Lord's Prayer: The preface in Matthew

What I have said, according to my capacity to receive the grace which has been given by God through his Christ, and as I trust in the Holy Spirit also—whether it be so, you will judge when you read it—may suffice by way of examination of the general subject of prayer. I shall now proceed to the next task, to consider how full of meaning is the prayer outlined by the Lord. It is first of all to be observed that to most people Matthew and Luke might seem to have recorded the same prayer sketched as a pattern for right prayer. Matthew's words run thus: "Our Father in heaven, hallowed be thy name. Thy kingdom come. Thy will be done, on earth as it is in heaven. Give us this day our daily bread. And forgive us our debts, as we also have forgiven our debtors. And do not bring us to the time of trial, but rescue us from the evil one" (Matthew 6:9–13). But Luke's run as follows: "Father, hallowed be thy name. Thy kingdom come. Give us each day our daily bread. And forgive us our sins, for we ourselves forgive everyone indebted to us. And do not bring us to the time of trial" (Luke 11:2–4).

To those who suppose it to be the same prayer, we may reply that the utterances, though they certainly resemble one another, also appear to differ, as I shall set forth in investigating them. In the second place it is not possible that the same prayer should be said on the mountain where, "When Jesus saw the crowds, he went up the mountain; and after he sat down, his disciples came to him. Then he began to speak, and taught them, saying"—for it is in the course of the recital of the Beatitudes and the subsequent injunctions that it is found recorded in Matthew. It also have been said, "He was praying in a certain place, and after he had finished, one of his disciples said to him, Lord, teach us to pray, as John taught his disciples."

It is surely impossible that the same words should be described as having been spoken in the course of continuous utterance without any question to precede them and as being announced in response to a disciple's request. One might, however, say the prayers are equivalent and were spoken as one. On the one occasion in continuous discourse, on the other in response to the request of a different disciple who in all likelihood was not present when he spoke the form in Matthew or had not mastered what had earlier been spoken. But perhaps it is better that the prayers be regarded as different, with certain portions in common.

In Mark, though I have searched there also, in case the record of an equivalent should escape me, I have not found so much as a vestige of a prayer contained. I have already said that before praying one must first be composed and disposed in a particular manner. Let us therefore glance at the words preceding the prayer contained in Matthew, which were uttered by our Savior. They are as follows: "And whenever you pray, do not be like the hypocrites; for they love to stand and pray in the synagogues and at the street corners, so that they may be seen by others.

Truly I tell you, they have received their reward. But whenever you pray, go into your room and shut the door and pray to your Father who is in secret; and your Father who sees in secret will reward you. When you are praying, do not heap up empty phrases as the Gentiles do; for they think that they will be heard because of their many words. Do not be like them, for your Father knows what you need before you ask him. Pray then in this way" (Matthew 6:5–9).

Our Savior often appears as inveighing against the love of glory as a deadly passion, just as he has done in this place where he dissuades us from the practice of actors at the season of prayer, for it is a practice of actors rather to plume themselves in piety before men rather than to have communion with God.

Remembering then the words, "How can you believe when you accept glory from one another and do not seek the glory that comes from the one who alone is God?" we ought to despise all glory with men, even though it be thought honorably gained, and to seek the strict and true glory which is from him alone who glorifies the deserving in a manner becoming to himself and exceeding the desert of the person glorified. The very act which would in itself be thought honorable and is thought praiseworthy is polluted when we do it to be glorified by men or to appear to men, and on that account it is attended by no recompense from God. Unerring as the whole of Jesus' language is, it becomes even more so when it is spoken with his accustomed oath.

Of those who for human glory seem to do good to their neighbor, or pray in synagogues and at broadway corners, he says. "Truly I tell you, they have received their reward." For as the rich man according to Luke had good things in his human life, being no longer capable of obtaining them after the present life because he had had them, so he that has his reward, as having sown not "unto the spirit" but "unto the flesh" shall "reap corruption" but shall not "reap eternal life" in his giving or in his prayers.

It is sowing unto the flesh when one does alms, with trumpeting before him, in synagogues and thoroughfares to be glorified by men, or likes to pray standing in synagogues and at broadway corners to appear to men and thought a pious and a holy person among the onlookers. Indeed every wayfarer along the broad and spacious way leading to destruction without rightness or straightness but crooked and cornered throughout (for the straight line is broken in it to the utmost) is standing no less than he who prays at broadway corners, not in one but through his love of pleasure in a number of streets in which beings, who as men are perishing because they have fallen away from their divinity, are to be found glorifying and pronouncing blessed those whom they have thought to act piously.

There are always many who are rather pleasure-loving than God-loving in their seeming prayer who debauch prayer amid banqueting and carousing, standing in truth at the broadway corners and praying. For everyone who has made pleasure his rule of life has in his passion for the spacious fallen out of the narrow straitened way of Jesus Christ that is without a single bend and has no corner at all.

There is a certain difference between Church and Synagogue. The church in the strict sense is without "a spot or wrinkle or anything of the kind" (Ephesians 5:27) is holy and blameless. Into it enters neither child of harlot, nor eunuch or emasenlate, nor yet Egyptian or Edomite unless sons born to them in the third generation enables them with difficulty to join the church, nor Moabite and Ammonite, unless the tenth generation is complete and the aeon passed.

The Synagogue, on the other hand, may be built by a centurion, as was the case in times preceding the sojourn of Jesus when as yet witness had not yet been borne that the man possessed faith such as the Son of God did not find even in Israel. Now he who likes to pray in synagogues is not far from broadway corners. But it is not so with the saint, for he loves, not likes, to pray in churches, not broadway corners, in the straightness of the narrow straitened way, not to appear to men, but to present himself before the Lord God, a male in the sense that he observes the acceptable year of the Lord and keeps the commandment which says, "Thrice in the year shall every male present himself before the Lord God" (Exodus 34:23).

We are to attend to the word "appear" carefully, since no appearance is a good inasmuch as it only seems to exist and not in truth, and misleads the senses and expresses nothing exactly and truly. As actors of plays in theaters are not what they profess nor are really what the mask they wear makes them look like, so too all who appear to assume the outward sensible form of goodness and are not righteous but actors of righteousness, acting moreover in a theater of their own—namely synagogues and broadway corners. But he that is no actor but has cast off all that is alien to him and sets himself to please in that theater which is inconceivably greater than any which has been mentioned, enters into his own storeroom to the riches therein treasured up, and shuts up after him his treasury of wisdom and knowledge.

Never turning his glance outwards or doting on things outside, having shut up every door of the senses that he may not be drawn away by sensations or have their sensible presentation stealing into his mind, prays to the Father who does not shun or desert a place so secret but dwells in it, the Only Begotten also being present with him. For he says "I and the Father will come unto him and make abode with him" (John 14:23). And plainly, if we do pray thus, we shall be interceding not only with a God but also with a Father who is righteous, who does not desert us as his children but is present in our secret place and watches it and increases the contents of the storeroom if we shut up its door.

When we pray let us not babble but use godly speech. We babble when, without scrutiny of ourselves or of the devotional words we are sending up, we speak of the corrupt in deed or word or thought, things which are mean and reprehensible and alien to the incorruptibleness of the Lord. He, then, that babbles in prayer is in a synagogic disposition worse than any yet described and in a harder way than those who are at broadway corners, preserving not as much as a vestige even of acting in goodness.

For according to the passage in the Gospel only heathen babble, being quite insensible of great or heavenly petitions and therefore sending up every prayer for the material and the external. To a babbling heathen,

then, is he like who asks for things below from the Lord who dwells in heaven and above the heights of the heavens.

He who is wordy also seems to be a babbler and he who babbles to be wordy. There is no unity in matter and in bodily substances, but every such supposed unity is split up and divided and disintegrated into many units to the loss of its union. Good is one; many are the base. Truth is one; many are the false. True righteousness is one; many are the states that act it as a part. God's wisdom is one; many are the wisdoms of this age and of the rulers of this age which come to nought. The word of God is one, but many are the words alien to God.

Therefore no one shall escape sin as the result of wordiness, and no one who thinks to be heard as the result of wordiness can be heard. For this reason we ought not to make our prayers like heathen babbling or wordiness or other practice after the likeness of the serpent, for the God of saints, being a Father, knows of what things his children have need, since such things are worthy of Fatherly knowledge.

He who knows not God knows not the things of God also—knows not the things of which he has need, for the things of which he thinks he has need are mistaken. But he who has contemplated the better and diviner things of which he is in need shall obtain the objects of his contemplation which are known by God and which have been known by the Father even before asking. After these remarks upon the preface to the prayer in the Gospel according to Matthew, let us now proceed to consider what the prayer sets forth.

CHAPTER 13

The Lord's Prayer—Our Father in Heaven

"Our Father in Heaven." It deserves a somewhat careful observation of the so-called Old Testament to discover whether it is possible to find anywhere in it a prayer of one who addresses God as Father. For though I have made examination to the best of my ability, I have up to the present failed to find one. I do not say that God is not spoken of as Father or that accounted believers in God are not called sons of God, but that I have not yet found in prayer that confidence in calling God Father which the Savior has proclaimed.

That God is spoken of as Father and those who have waited on God's word as sons, may be seen in many places, as in Deuteronomy, "You have forsaken God your parent and forgotten God your nourisher" (Deuteronomy 32:18), and again, "Is he not your Father himself that got you and made you and created you?" (Deuteronomy 32:6); and again, "Sons who have not faith in them" (Deuteronomy 32:20). And in Isaiah, "I have nourished and brought up children, and they have rebelled against me" (Isaiah 1:2); and in Malachi, "A son honors his father, and a servant his master: if then I be a father, where is my honor? And if I be a master, where is my fear?" (Malachi 1:6). So then, even though God is termed Father and their Sons who have been begotten by reason of their faith in him, yet sure and unchangeable sonship is not to be seen in the ancient people.

The very passages I have cited since the subjection of those so-called sons, since according to the apostle "the heir, as long as he is a child, differs nothing from a servant, though he be lord of all; but is under tutors and governors until the time appointed of the father" (Galatians 4:1–2). But the fullness of time is in the sojourn of our Lord Jesus Christ, when they who desire receive adoption as sons, as Paul teaches in the words, "For you did not receive a spirit of slavery unto fear, but you received a spirit of adoption as sons, wherein we cry Abba, Father" (Galatians 4:6); and as it is in the Gospel according to John, "To as many as received him he gave authority to become children of God if believers on his name" (John 1:12); and it is by reason of this Spirit of adoption as sons, we learn in the Catholic Epistle of John regarding the begotten of God, that "Everyone that is begotten of God does no sin because his seed abides in him, and he cannot sin because he is begotten of God" (1 John 5:18).

And yet if we think of the meaning of the words which are written in Luke, "When you pray say, Father," etc., we shall hesitate to address this expression to him unless we have become genuine sons in case, in addition to our other sins, we should also become liable to a charge of impiety. My meaning is as follows. In the first Epistle to Corinthians Paul says, "No one can say Jesus is Lord save in a holy spirit, and no one that speaks in God's spirit says cursed be Jesus, calling the same thing a holy spirit and God's spirit" (1 Corinthians 12:3). What is meant by speaking in a holy spirit of Jesus as Lord is not quite clear, as countless actors and numbers of heterodox people, and at times even demons conquered by the power in the name, utter the expression.

No one therefore will venture to declare that anyone of these calls Jesus Lord in a holy spirit. For the same reason, indeed, they could not be shown to call Jesus Lord at all, since they alone call Jesus Lord who express it from inward disposition in service to the word of God and in proclaiming no other Lord than him in all their conduct. And if it be such who say Jesus is Lord, it may be that everyone who sins, in that he curses the divine Word through his transgression, has through his actions called out, "Cursed be Jesus."

And accordingly, as the one type of man says "Jesus is Lord," and the man of opposite disposition "Cursed be Jesus," "so everyone that has been begotten of God and does not sin," because he is partaker of God's seed which turns him from all sin, says through his conduct "Our Father in Heaven," the spirit himself witnessing with their spirit that they are children of God and heirs to him and joint heirs with Christ, since as suffering with him they reasonably hope with him also to be glorified. But in order that theirs may be no one-sided utterance of the words "Our Father," in addition to their actions they have a heart—a fountain and source of good actions—believing unto righteousness, in harmony with which their mouth makes acknowledgment unto salvation.

So then their every act and word and thought, formed by the only begotten Word in accord with him, imitates the image of the invisible God and has come to be "in accordance with the image of the Creator" who makes "the sun to rise upon evil men and good, and rains upon righteous and unrighteous" (Matthew 5:45) that there may be in them the image of the heavenly One who is himself also an image of God. Saints, therefore, as an image of an Image himself, a son, receive the impress of Sonship, becoming conformed not only to the glorified body of Christ but also to him who is in that body, and they become conformed to him who is in a glorified body through being transformed by the renewing of their mind.

And if such men through out the whole of life voice the words "Our Father in the Heavens," plainly he that does sin, as John says in the Catholic Epistle, "is of the devil because the devil sins from the beginning" (1 John 3:8), and just as God's seed abiding in the begotten of God produces inability to sin in him who is formed in accordance with the only begotten Word, so the devil's seed is in everyone that does sin, to the extent in which it is present within the soul—not suffering its possessor to have power to prosper. But since "for this end was the Son of God manifested that he might undo the actions of the devil" (1 John 3:8), it is possible, through the undoing of the actions of the devil by the sojourn of the Word of God within our Soul, for the evil seed implanted in us to be utterly removed and for us to become children of God.

Let us, therefore, not think that it is words we are taught to say in any appointed season of prayer. On the contrary, if we understand our former consideration of prayer without ceasing, let our whole life of prayer without ceasing speak the words "Our Father in the Heavens," having its commonwealth in no wise on earth but in every way in heaven, which is God's throne because of the foundation of the kingdom of God in all who wear the image of the Heavenly One and therefore become heavenly. When the Father of saints is said to be in the heavens, we are not to suppose that he is circumscribed by material form and dwells in heaven.

Since, in that case, as contained God will be formed to be less than the heavens because they contain him, whereas the ineffable might of his godhead demands our belief that all things are contained and held together by him. And, in general, passages which taken literally are thought by the simpler order of minds to assert that God is in space are to be otherwise taken in a sense more becoming to great spiritual concepts of God.

Such are those passages in the Gospel according to John: "Before the feast of the Passover, Jesus, knowing that his hour had come that he should pass from this world to the Father, as he had loved his own who were in the world, loved them to the end" (John 13:1); and shortly after: "Knowing that the Father had given all into his hands, and that he had come forth from God and was returning to God" (John 13:3); and later: "You heard that I said to you, I return and come unto you. If you loved me you would have rejoiced that I go to the Father" (John 14:28); and again later: "Now I return to him that sent me, and none of you asks me: Where do you return?" (John 16:5).

If these things are to be taken spatially, so also plainly is: "Jesus answered and said to them, If any one love me he will keep my word and my Father will love him and we shall come unto him and make abode with him" (John 14:23). But surely the words do not imply a spacial transition of the Father and the Son to the lover of the word of Jesus and are therefore not to be taken spatially.

On the contrary, the Word of God, in condescension for us and, in regard to his proper desert, in humiliation while among men, is said to pass from this world unto the Father so that we also may behold him perfectly there in reversion to his proper fullness from the emptiness among us whereby he emptied himself—where we also, enjoying his guidance, shall be filled and freed from all emptiness. To such an end the Word of God well may leave the world and depart to him that sent him, and go to the Father! And as for that passage near the end of the Gospel according to John, "Cling not to me, for I am not yet gone up unto my Father" (John 20:17), let us seek to conceive it in the more mystical sense.

Let ours be the more reverent conception of the ascension of the Son to the Father with sanctified insight, an ascension rather of soul than of body. I think it right to have linked these considerations to the clause "Our Father in the Heavens" for the sake of doing away with a low conception of God held by those who think that he is in heaven spatially, and of preventing anyone from saying God is in material space since it follows that he also is physical, which leads to opinions most impious—to belief that he is divisible and material and corruptible. For every material thing is divisible and corruptible.

Or else let them tell us, not on the strength of vague sensation but with a claim to clear understanding, how it can be of any other than a material nature. Since, then, in writings before Christ's bodily sojourn there are also many statements which seem to say that God is in physical space, it appears to me to be not out of place to cite a few of them also for the sake of doing away with any doubt in those who, because they know no better, confine God, who is over all, within small and scanty space on their own scale.

First, in Genesis it says Adam and Eve heard the sound of the lord God walking at evening in the garden, and both Adam and his wife hid themselves from the Lord God amid the wood of the Garden. I shall put the question to those who not only refuse to enter into the treasures of the passage but do not so much as knock at all at its door, whether they are able to imagine the Lord God, who fills the heaven and the earth, who as they themselves suppose in the more physical sense uses heaven as throne and the earth as a footstool for his feet, as contained by so scanty a space in comparison with the whole heaven and the earth that a garden which they suppose to be material is not filled by God but so far exceeds him in greatness as to hold him even when walking while a sound from the tread of his feet is heard? Absurder still on their interpretation is the hiding of Adam and Eve, in fear of God by reason of their transgression, from before God amid the wood of the Garden.

For it is not even said that they merely desired to hide, but that they actually hid themselves. And how is it in their view that God inquires of Adam saying, "Where are you?" I have discussed these matters at greater length in my examination of the contents of Genesis, yet here, too—in order not to pass by so grave a subject in complete silence—it will suffice if I recall what is said by God in Deuteronomy: "I will dwell in them and walk in them" (Exodus 29:45; Leviticus 26:12). For as is his walk in saints, such is his walk in the Garden also, since everyone that sins hides from God and shuns his oversight and renounces his confidence with him. So it was that Cain also went out from before God and dwelt in the land of Nod over against Eden. In the same way, therefore, as he dwells in saints.

So also does he dwell in heaven (that is, in every saint who wears the image of the Heavenly One, or Christ, in whom all who are being saved are luminaries and stars of heaven, or else because saints are in heaven) according to the saying: "Unto you who dwells in heaven have I lifted up my eyes" (Psalm 123:1). And yet the passage in Ecclesiastes, "Be not in haste to utter speech before God, because God is in heaven above, and you on Earth below" (Ecclesiastes 5:2), means to show the interval which separates those who are in the body of humiliation from him who is with the angels and holy powers who are being exalted by the help of the Word also and with Christ himself. For it is not unreasonable that he should be strictly at the Father's throne, allegorically called heaven, while his church, termed Earth, is a footstool at his feet.

I have cited a few Old Testament utterances, thought to represent God in space, for the sake of urging the reader by every means within the power given me to accept the divine scripture in the higher and more spiritual sense whenever it seems to teach that God is in space. And it was fitting that these considerations should be linked to the clause Our Father in the Heavens inasmuch as it distinguishes the essence of God from all created beings. For it is upon such as do not share in that essence that a certain glory of God and a power from him, an outflow of the deity, comes.

CHAPTER 14

Hallowed be thy name

"Hallowed be thy name." Although this may represent either that the object of prayer has not yet come to pass, or after its attainment, that it is not permanent in which case the request is for its retention; the lan-

guage in this instance makes it plain that it is with the implication that
the name of the Father has not yet been hallowed, that we are bidden—
according to Matthew and Luke, that is—to say "Hallowed be thy name."
Then how, one might say, should a man request the hallowing of God's
name as though not hallowed? Let us understand what the Father's name,
and what the hallowing of it, means. A name is a summary designation
descriptive of the peculiar character of the thing named.

Thus the Apostle Paul has a certain peculiar character, partly of
soul which is accordingly of a certain kind, partly of intellect which is
accordingly contemplative of certain things, and partly of body which is
accordingly of a certain kind. It is the peculiar in these characteristics,
the unique combination—for there is not another being identical with
Paul—that is indicated by means of the appellation "Paul." In the case of
men, however, whose peculiar characteristics are changed, their names
also by a sound usage are changed according to scripture.

When the character of Abram was transformed, he was called Abraham; when that of Simon he was named Peter, and when that of Saul
the persecutor of Jesus, he was designated Paul. But in the case of God,
inasmuch as he is himself ever unchangeable and unalterable, the proper
name which even he may be said to bear is ever one, that mentioned in
Exodus, "He that is," or the like. Since therefore, though we all have some
notion of God, conceiving of him in various ways, but not all of what he
is, for few and, be it said, fewer than few are they who comprehend his
compete holiness—we are with good reason taught to attain to a holy
conception of him in order that we may see his holiness as creator, pro-
vider, judge, elector, abandoner, acceptor, rejector, rewarder and punisher
of each according to his desert.

For it is in such and similar terms that God's peculiar character may
be said to be sketched which I take to be the meaning of the expression,
God's name according to the scriptures in Exodus, "You shall not take the
name of the Lord your God in vain" (Exodus 20:7); in Deuteronomy, "Be
my utterance awaited as rain: as dew let my words descend, as showers
upon herbage and as moisture upon grass: for I have called on the Lord's

name" (Deuteronomy 30:2); and in Psalms, "They shall remember your name in every generation" (Psalm 45:17).

It is he who associates the thought of God with wrong things that takes the name of the Lord God in vain, and he who is able to utter rain that cooperates with his hearers in the fruit bearing of their souls, and who addresses words of exhortation that are like dew, and who in the edifying torrent of his words turns upon his listeners showers most helpful or moisture most efficacious, is able to do so because he has perceived his need of God as the accomplisher, and calls in the real supplier of those things; and everyone who penetrates the very things of God recalls to mind rather than learns the mysteries of piety, even when he seems to be told them by another or thinks that he discovers them. And as the suppliant ought at this point to reflect that his asking is for the hallowing of God's name, so in Psalms it is said, "Let us exalt his name together" (Psalm 34:3), the patriarch enjoining attainment to the true and exalted knowledge of God's peculiar nature with all harmony, in the same mind, and in the same will.

It is exalting the name of God together when, after one has participated in an outflow of deity in having been sustained by God and having overcome his enemies so that they are unable to rejoice over his fall, he exalts the power of God in which he has participated, as is shown in the [thirtieth] psalm by the words, "I will exalt you, O Lord, for you have sustained me and not made my enemies to rejoice over me" (Psalm 30:2). A man exalts God when he has consecrated to him a house within himself, since the superscription of the Psalm also runs thus: "A Psalm of singing for the consecration of the House of David."

It is further to be observed regarding the clause "Hallowed be thy name" and its successors in imperative form, that the translators also continually made use of imperatives instead of ablatives, as in the Psalms: "Speechless let the guileful lips be, that speak lawlessness against the righteous" (Psalm 31:18) instead of "may they be," and "Let the creditor search out all his possessions," "Let him possess no helper" (Psalm 109:11–12) concerning Judas in the one hundred and [ninth]; for the whole Psalm is a petition concerning Judas that certain things may befall him.

But Tatian, failing to perceive that "let" there be does not always signify the ablative but is occasionally also imperative, has most impiously supposed that God said, "Let there be light," in prayer rather than in command that the light should be; since, as he puts it in his godless thought, God was in darkness. In reply to him it may be asked, how is he going to take the other sayings? "Let the Earth grow grass," and "Let the water below heaven be gathered together," and "Let the waters bring forth creeping things with living souls," and "Let the earth bring forth a living soul" (Genesis 1). Is it for the sake of standing upon firm ground that he prays that the water below heaven be gathered together into one meeting place, or for the sake of partaking of the things that grow from the earth that he prays, "Let the Earth grow," etc.?

What manner of need, to match his need of light; has he of creatures of water, air, and land that he should pray for them also? If even on Tatian's view it is absurd to think of him as praying for these things which occur in imperative expressions, may the same not be said of "Let be there light"—that it is an imperative and not an ablative expression? I thought that, in view of the fact that prayer is expressed in imperative forms, some reference was necessary to his perversion for the sake of those—I myself have met with cases who have been misled into accepting his impious teaching.

CHAPTER 15

Thy kingdom come

"Thy kingdom come." According to the word of our Lord and Savior, the kingdom of God does not come observably, nor shall men say, "Lo it is here," or, "Lo is it there," but the kingdom of God is within us (Luke 17:21); for the utterance is exceedingly near in our mouth and in our heart. It is therefore plain that he who prays for the coming of the kingdom of God prays with good reason for rising and fruit bearing and perfecting of God's kingdom within him.

For every saint is ruled over by God and obeys the Spiritual laws of God, and conducts himself like a well-ordered city; and the Father is present with him, and Christ rules together with the Father in the perfected Soul, according to the saying that I mentioned shortly before, "We will come unto him and make abode with him" (John 14:23). By God's kingdom, I understand the blessed condition of the mind and the settled order of wise reflection; by Christ's kingdom, the issue of words of salvation to their hearers and the practice of acts of righteousness and the other excellences; for the son of God is Word and righteousness.

But every sinner is tyrannized by the ruler of this world, since every sinner is in conformity with the present evil world and does not yield himself to him who gave himself for us sinners, that he might release us from the present evil world and release us according to the will of God our Father, as it is expressed in the Epistle to Galatians. And he who, by reason of deliberate sin is tyrannized by the ruler of this world, is also ruled over by sin: wherefore we are bidden by Paul to be no longer subject to sin that would rule over us, and we are enjoined in these words: "Let sin therefore not rule in our mortal body that we should obey its lusts" (Romans 6:12).

But in reference to both clauses, "Hallowed be thy name" and "Thy kingdom come," it may be urged that, if the suppliant prays them with a view to being heard and ever is heard, plainly his will be an instance, answering to what has just been said, of the name of God being hallowed and of the rise of the kingdom of God, in which event how shall he any longer with propriety pray for things already present as though they not present, saying, "Hallowed be thy name; thy kingdom come"? And in that case, it will sometimes be proper *not* to say, "Hallowed be thy name; thy kingdom come."

To this it may be replied that just as he who prays to obtain a word of knowledge and a word of wisdom will with propriety pray for them continually, with the prospect of continually receiving fuller contemplations of wisdom and knowledge through being heard, although his knowledge of such things as he may be able in the present to receive is partial, whereas the perfect that annuls the partial shall then be manifested when the mind confronts its objects face to face without sensation—so perfection in our individual hallowing of the name of God and in the rise of his kingdom within us is not possible unless there also come perfection of knowledge and wisdom and it may be the other excellences.

We are wayfaring toward perfection if we forget the things behind, pressing on toward those before us. The kingdom of God within us will therefore be consummated in us as we advance without ceasing, when, the saying in the Apostle is fulfilled, that Christ, his enemies all made subject to him, shall deliver the kingdom to God the Father that God may be All in All (1 Corinthians 15:28). For this reason, let us pray without ceasing with a disposition made divine by the Word, and say to our Father in heaven, "Hallowed be thy name; thy kingdom come." Of the kingdom of God it is further to be said by way of distinction that as righteousness has no partnership with lawlessness and light no community with darkness and Christ no argument with Belial, so a kingdom of sin is incompatible with the kingdom of God.

If, accordingly, we would be ruled over by God, by no means let sin rule in our mortal body, nor let us obey its commands when it calls our soul forth to the works of the flesh that are alien to God, but let us mortify our members that are on earth and bear the fruits of the Spirit, that the Lord may walk in us as in a spiritual garden, ruling alone over us with his Christ seated within us on the right of the Spiritual power that we pray to receive, sitting until all his enemies within us become a footstool for his feet and every rule and authority and power be undone from us.

These things may come to pass in the case of each of us, and death the last energy be undone, so that Christ may say within us also: "O death, where is your sting? O grave, where is your victory?" (1 Corinthians 15:55). Even now, therefore, let our corruptible put on the holiness and incorruptibleness that consists in chastity and purity, and our mortal, death undone, wrap itself in the paternal immortality, so that, being ruled over by God, we may even now live amid the blessings of regeneration and resurrection.

CHAPTER 16

Thy will be done on earth also as in heaven

"Thy will be done on earth also as in heaven." After the clause "thy king-dom come," Luke has passed over these words in silence and placed the clause "Give us daily our needful bread." Let us therefore examine next in succession the words I have placed first, as set down in Matthew alone. As suppliants who are still on earth, believing that the will of God is done in heaven among all the household of the heavens, let us pray that the will of God may be done by us also who are on earth in like manner with them, as will come to pass when we do nothing contrary to his will.

And when the will of God as it is in heaven has been accomplished by us also who are on earth, we shall inherit a kingdom of heaven as having, alike with them, worn the image of the Heavenly One, while those who come after us on earth are praying to become in turn like us who have come to be in heaven.

So far as Matthew alone is concerned, the words "on earth also as in heaven" can be taken in common, so that what we are enjoined to say in prayer would run thus: "Hallowed be thy name on earth also as in heaven; thy kingdom come on earth also as in heaven; thy will be done on earth also as in heaven." For alike the name of God has been hallowed among those who are in heaven, and the kingdom of God is risen in them, and the will of God has been done in their midst—things indeed which are all unrealized by us but which can be acquired by us through rendering ourselves worthy to obtain God's hearing in reference to them all.

The words "Thy will be done on earth also as in heaven" may raise the question how has the will of God been done in heaven where the spiritual forces of evil are, by reason of which the sword of God shall drink deep even in heaven? If we pray thus, that the will of God be done on earth just as it is being done in heaven, may we not thoughtlessly be praying that the very opposite may abide on earth where such things already come from heaven, since much that is bad on earth is due to the overcoming spiritual forces of evil which are in the heavenly places?

Anyone who allegorizes heaven and asserts that it is Christ, and earth the church—what throne so worthy of the Father as Christ? What footstool of the feet of God as the Church?—will easily solve the question by replying that everyone in the church ought to pray to receive the paternal will in such wise as Christ has done, who came to do the will of his Father and accomplished if completely. For it is possible by being joined to him to become one spirit with him and therefore receptive of the will to the end that, as it has been accomplished in heaven, so it may be accomplished on earth also; for he that is joined to the Lord, according to Paul, is one spirit (1 Corinthians 6:17). And I believe that one who carefully considers it will find this an interpretation not to be despised.

But someone may dispute it by citing what is said to the eleven disciples by the Lord after the resurrection at the close of the this gospel: "There has been given to me all authority on earth also as in heaven" (Matthew 28:18). That is, having authority over the things that are in heaven, he says that he has also received it over those on earth. Whereas those that are in heaven have already been illumined by the Word, it is at the consummation of the world that those on earth are also, in imitation of those over which the Savior received authority, brought to a successful issue by reason of the authority given to the Son of God. Accordingly his will is to receive those who are disciples under him as in a sense cooperants through their prayers to the Father in order that, in like manner with the things in heaven that are subject to Truth and Word, he may lead the things on earth, restored by reason of the authority which he has received on earth also as in heaven, to an end fraught with bliss for the objects of his authority.

On the other hand one who would take heaven to be the Savior and earth the church, asserting that it is the firstborn of all creation, on whom the Father reposes as on a throne, that is heaven, would find that it is the man whom he put on after having been fitted for such power because he had humbled himself and having been obedient till death, who says after the resurrection, "There has been given to me all authority on earth also as in heaven"—the man in the Savior having received his authority over the things in heaven, as the proper possessions of the Only-begotten, in order to be in communion with him, mingling in his divinity and becoming one with him.

But if this second thought does not yet solve the difficulty as to how the will of God can be in heaven when the spiritual forces of evil in the heavenly places wrestle against those who are on earth, it will be possible to solve the question from this consideration: It is not by virtue of place but of principle that one who is still on earth but has a commonwealth in heaven and lays up treasure in heaven and has his heart in heaven and wears the image of the Heavenly One, is no longer of the earth nor of the world below but of heaven and of the heavenly world that is better than this.

So, too, the spiritual forces of evil which still dwell in the heavenly places but have their commonwealth on earth and plot against men the means whereby they wrestle against mankind, and lay up treasure on earth, and wear an image of the Earthly One who the beginning of the Lord's fashioning made to be mocked by the angels, are not heavenly nor by reason of their vicious disposition do they dwell in the heavens. Accordingly when it is said, "Thy will be done on earth also as in heaven," we are not to reckon those beings as in heaven at all, because through pride they have fallen along with him who fell from heaven like a thunderbolt.

And it may well be that our Savior, in saying that we ought to pray that the Father's will may be done on earth also as in heaven, does not by any means order prayer for things spatially on earth that they may be made like things spatially in heaven, but his will in enjoining prayer is that all things on earth—that is, things inferior and conformed to the earthly—be made like the better, which have their commonwealth in heaven, which have all become heaven.

For he that sins, wherever he may be, is earth, and will turn into the like somehow, unless he repents, whereas he that does the will of God and does not disobey the spiritual laws of salvation is heaven. Whether therefore we are still earth because of sin, let us pray that the will of God may extend restoringly to us also as it has already reached those who have become or are heaven before us; or if we are already accounted not earth but heaven by God, let our request be that, in like manner with heaven, on earth also, in inferior things I mean, the will of God may be fulfilled unto what I may term earth's heaven-making, so that there shall be no longer earth but all things become heaven.

For if, on this interpretation, the will of God be done on earth also as in heaven, earth will not remain earth, just as to make my meaning clearer with another illustration: If the will of God be done in the case of the wanton as it has been with the temperate, the wanton will be temperate, or if it should be in the case of the unrighteous as it has been with the righteous, the unrighteous will be righteous. If, therefore, the will of God be done on earth also as it has been in heaven, we shall all be heaven; for though flesh that helps not; and blood that is akin to it, are unable to inherit God's kingdom, they may be said to inherit it if they be changed from flesh and earth and clay and blood to the heavenly essence.

CHAPTER 17
Give us today our needful bread

"Give us today our needful bread," or as Luke has it, "Give us daily our needful bread." Seeing that some suppose that it is meant that we should pray for material bread, their erroneous opinion deserves to be done away with and the truth about the needful bread set forth, in the following manner. We may put the question to them: How can it be that he, who says that heavenly and great things ought to be asked for as if, on their view, he has forgotten his teaching now enjoins the offering of intercession to the Father for an earthly and little thing, since neither is the bread which is assimilated into our flesh a heavenly thing nor is it asking a great thing to request it?

For my part, I shall follow the Teacher's own teaching as to the bread and cite the passages in detail. To men who have come to Capernaum to seek him he says, in the Gospel according to John, "Verily, verily, I tell you, you seek me not because you saw signs but because you ate of the loaves of bread and were filled" (John 6:26), for he that has eaten and been filled with the loaves of bread which have been blessed by Jesus seeks the more to grasp the Son of God more closely and hastens toward him.

Wherefore he will enjoin: "Work not for the food that perishes but for the food that abides unto life eternal, which the Son of Man shall give you" (John 6:27). And when, upon that, they who had heard inquired and said: "What are we to do that we may work the works of God?" Jesus answered and said to them: "This is the work of God, that you believe on him whom he has sent" (John 6:28–29). As it is written in Psalms, "God sent his Word and healed them" (Psalm 107:20), that is the diseased, and believers in that Word work the works of God which are food that abides unto life eternal.

And my Father, he says, gives you the true bread from heaven, for the bread of God is that which comes down from heaven and gives life to the world. It is true bread that nourishes the true man who is made in God's image, and he that has been nourished by it also becomes in the Creator's likeness. What is more nourishing to the soul than Word, or what more precious to the mind of him that is capable of receiving it than the Wisdom of God?

What is more congenial to the rational nature than Truth? Should it be urged in objection to this view that he would not in that case teach men to ask for needful bread as if something other than himself, it is to be noted that he also discourses in the Gospel according to John sometimes as if it were other than himself but at other times as if he is himself the Bread. The former in the sense of the words: "Moses has given you the bread from heaven yet not the true bread, but my Father gives you the true bread from heaven" (John 6:32).

In the latter sense, to those who had said to him, "Ever give us this bread," he says: "I am the bread of life: he that comes unto me shall not hunger, and he that believes on me shall not thirst"; and shortly after: "I am the living bread that is come down from heaven: if anyone eat of this bread he shall live unto eternity: yea and the bread which I shall give is my flesh which I shall give for the sake of the life of the world" (John 6:48–58).

Now since all manner of nourishment is spoken of as bread according to Scripture, as is clear from the fact that it is recorded of Moses that he ate not bread and drank not water forty days, and since the nourishing Word is manifold and various, not all being capable of nourishment by the solidity and strength of the divine teachings, he is therefore pleased to offer strenuous nourishment befitting men more perfect, where he says: "The bread which I shall give is my flesh which I shall give for the sake of the life of the world": and shortly after: "Except you eat the flesh of the son of Man and drinks his blood, you have not life in yourselves. He that eats my flesh and drinks my blood has life eternal, and I will raise him up in the last day. For my flesh is true food and my blood is true drink. He that eats my flesh and drinks my blood abides in me and I in him. As the living Father sent me and I live because of the Father, so also he that eats me—he too shall live because of me" (John 6). This is the true food, Christ's flesh, which being Word has become flesh, as it is said, "And the Word became flesh" (John 1:14). When we eat and drink the Word, he tabernacles in us.

When he is assimilated the words are fulfilled, "We beheld his glory" (John 1:14). This is the bread that is come down from heaven. Not as the fathers ate and died, he that eats this bread shall live unto eternity. Discoursing to infant Corinthians who walk in the way of man, Paul says: "I gave you milk to drink, not meat, for you were not yet able. Nay even now you are not yet able, for you are still of the flesh" (1 Corinthians 3:2); and in the Epistle to Hebrews: "And you are become in need of milk, not of solid nourishment. For anyone who partakes of milk is devoid of moral reason, for he is infant" (Hebrews 5:12–13).

But solid nourishment is for mature men who by force of use have their senses trained to discriminate good and evil. In my opinion the words "One man has faith to eat anything, but he that is weak eats vegetables" (Romans 14:2) are also in his intention meant to refer not to material forms of nourishment but to the words of God that nourish the soul: Of these the man most faithful and mature is able to partake of any, he being denoted in the words One man has faith to eat anything, whereas the weaker and more immature is content with simpler teachings that do not quite produce full strength in him, reference being intended to him in the words "But he that is weak eats vegetables."

There is also in Solomon a saying in the Proverbs, which I think teaches that the man who by reason of simplicity is incapable of the stronger and greater sentiments is better, short of false thought, than the man who, though more ready and keener and of greater insight into things, fails to penetrate the principle of peace and harmony in all. Solomon's passage runs as follows: "Better is hospitality of vegetables served with friendship and grace than a fatted calf with enmity" (Proverbs 15:17).

Many a time do we accept untutored simpler entertainment, accompanied by good conscience, as guests at the table of those who are unable to furnish us with more, with greater satisfaction than any elevation of words upreared against the knowledge of God and proclaiming with ample plausibility a sentiment alien to the Father of our Lord Jesus, who has given the law and the prophets. In order, therefore, that we may neither fall sick of soul for lack of nourishment nor die to God because of famine of the Lord's word, let us in obedience to the teaching of our Savior, with righter faith and life, ask the Father for the living bread which is the same as the needful bread.

Let us now consider what the word *epiousion*, "needful," means. First of all it should be known that the word *epiousion* is not found in any Greek writer whether in philosophy or in common usage, but seems to have been formed by the evangelists. At least Matthew and Luke, in having given it to the world, concur in using it in identical form. The same thing has been done by translators from Hebrew in other instances also; for what Greek ever used the expression *enotizou* or *akoutisthete* instead of *eistaota dexai* or *akousai poice se*.

Exactly like the expression *epiousion*, needful, is one found in Moses' writings, spoken by God: "You shall be my *periousios*—peculiar people"

(Deuteronomy 14:2; 26:18). Either word seems to me to be a compound of *ousia*—"essence"—the former signifying the bread that contributes to the essence, the latter denoting the people that has to do with the essence and is associated with it. As for *ousia*, "essence," in the strict sense, by those who assert the priority of the substance of immaterial things, it is ranked with immaterial things which are in possession of permanent being and neither receive addition nor suffer subtraction. For addition and subtraction are characteristic of material things in reference to which growth and decay take place owing to their being in a state of flux, in need of imported support and nourishment.

If the import exceeds the waste in a period growth takes place, if it is less, diminution; and if, as in conceivable, there are things receiving no import at all, they are in what I may term unmitigated diminution. Those, on the other hand, who hold the substance of immaterial things to be posterior and that of material things to be prior, define essence in these terms: It is the primary matter of existing things out of which they are or the matter of bodily things out of which they are; or that of terms out of which they are; or the primary unqualified substance or presubstance of existing things; or that which admits of all transformations and modifications though itself as such inherently incapable of modification; or that which undergoes all modification and transformation.

On their view essence is inherently unqualified and inarticulate as such. It is even indeterminate in magnitude, but it is involved in all quality as a kind of ready ground for it. By qualities they mean distinctively like the actualities and the activities in which movements and articulations of the essence have come to be, and they say that the essence as such has no part in these inherently though it is always incidentally inseparable from some of them and equally receptive of all the agent's actualizations however it may act and transform. (For it the force associated with the essence, pervading all that would be responsible for all quality and the particular dispositions involving it.)

And they say that it is throughout transformable and throughout divisible, and that any essence can coalesce with any other, all being a unity not withstanding. What I have said in this discussion of essence raised by the expressions the needful bread and the peculiar people has been to distinguish the meanings of "essence." And since we have already seen that it is spiritual bread for which we ought to ask, we must needs understand the essence to be akin to the bread, so that just as material bread on assimilation into the body of the nourished passes into its essence, so the living bread which is come down from heaven being assimilated into the mind and soul may impart its own power to him who has lent himself to nourishment from it, and so become the needful bread for which we ask.

And again, in like manner, as the nourished attains strength varying according to the character of the nourishment whether solid and fit for athletes or of the nature of milk and vegetables, so it follows that when the word of God is given either as milk as befits children, or as vegetables as suits invalids, or as flesh as is proper for combatants, each of the nourished acquires this or that power or nature according to the word to which he has lent himself.

Moreover, there is a kind of reputed nourishment which is in reality harmful, a second that is productive of disease, and another that cannot even be assimilated, and all of these may be transferred by analogy to varieties of reputedly nourishing teachings. Needful, therefore, is the bread which corresponds most closely to our rational nature and is akin to our very essence, which invests the soul at once with well-being and with strength, and, since the Word of God is immortal, imparts to its eater its own immortality.

It is just this needful bread that seems to me to be otherwise termed in Scripture a "tree of life," he who stretches forth his hand to which and takes of it shall live unto eternity. And under a third name this tree is termed "wisdom of God" in Solomon's words: "She is a tree of life to all that take hold upon her, and to those that lean upon her as upon the Lord she is safe" (Proverbs 3:18). And since the angels also are nourished by God's wisdom receiving power for the accomplishment of their proper works from their contemplation in truth with wisdom, it is said in Psalms that the angels also are nourished, men of God designated Hebrews holding communion with the angels and, as it were, even becoming mess fellows with them.

Such is the meaning of the saying, "Bread of angels has man eaten" (Psalm 78:25). Far from us be such poverty of mind as to suppose that it is of some material bread, such as is recorded to have come down from heaven upon those who had quitted Egypt, that the angels continually partake and are nourished, as though it was actually in this that the Hebrews had communion with the angels, God's ministering spirits. And while we are considering the needful bread and the tree of life and the wisdom of God and the common nourishment of saintly men and angels, it is not untimely to refer to the three men recorded in Genesis who were entertained by Abraham and partook of three measures of fine flour of wheat kneaded into ember cakes, and to observe that this may perhaps simply be told in a figurative sense.

It would show that saints are able upon occasion to impart spiritual and rational nourishment not only to men but also to divine powers, either for their benefit or for the exhibition of their most nourishing acquisitions, the angels being cheered and nourished in such display and becoming the readier to cooperate in every way and henceforth to conspire in the apprehension of fuller and greater things by the man who has cheered and so to say nourished them with his store of nourishing teachings already acquired.

No wonder that a man may nourish angels when even Christ avows himself to stand before the door and knock, in order that he may enter into him that opens to him and sup with him on his fare, thereafter himself in turn to impart his own to him who first according to his individual power has entertained the Son of God. So then the partaker of the needful bread, having his heart confirmed, becomes a son of God, whereas he that has portion in the serpent is none other than a spiritual Ethiopian and himself in turn changes into a snake by reason of the serpent's toils so that, even should he express a desire for baptism, he is reproached by the Word and hears it said: "Snakes, offspring of vipers, who has prompted you to flee from the coming wrath?" (Matthew 3:7).

And David speaks of the serpent body being fed on by Ethiopians: "You have shattered the heads of the serpents in the water, you have crushed the serpent's head, you have given him to be food for the Ethiopian peoples." If it is not absurd to suppose that, since the Son of God and also the Adversary are of essential substances, either of them may become nourishment to this soul or that, why need we hesitate in the case of all powers, better and worse, including human beings, to believe that each one of us may derive nourishment from any of them?

As Peter was about to commune with the centurion Cornelius and those who met together with him in Caesarea, and thereafter to impart the words of God to the Gentiles also, he saw the vessel let down from heaven by four corners, in which were all manner of quadrupeds and reptiles and beasts of the earth, whereupon he was also bidden rise up and stay and eat, and after he had said in deprecation, "You know that nothing common or unclean has ever entered my mouth" (Acts 10:14), he was commanded to call no man common or unclean because what God had made clean ought not to be made common by Peter; in the words of the passage, what things God has made clean, do not make common.

Accordingly, the clean and unclean food distinguished according to the law of Moses in terms of various animals bear an analogy to the differing characters of rational beings and teaches that some are nourishing for us but others the reverse until God has cleansed and made all, or those from every race, nourishing. But while that is indeed so and while there is such diversity among foods, the needful bread, for which we ought to pray in order to be counted worthy of it, and, being nourished by the Word that was God with God in the beginning to be made divine God, is one and transcends all the foods mentioned.

But it will be said that the word *epiousion*, "needful," is formed from *epienai*, to go on, so that we are bidden to ask for the bread proper to the coming age, in order that God may take it in advance and bestow it on us now. Thus what was to be given as it were tomorrow would be given us today, today being taken to mean the present age, tomorrow the coming. Since, however, as far as I can judge, the preceding interpretation is better, let us go on to consider the added reference to today in Matthew or the expression daily written in Luke.

To call the whole present age "today" is a usage frequent in the Scriptures, as in the passages, "He is father of the Moabites until today" (Genesis 19:37) and "He is father of the Ammonites until today" (Genesis 19:38) and "This account has been reported among Jews until today" (Matthew 28:15) and in the Psalms, "Today if you hear his voice, harden not your hearts" (Psalm 95:7–8). In Joshua, this is expressed very clearly: "Turn not away from the Lord in the days of today" (Joshua 22:18).

And if "today" means the whole present age, "yesterday" is probably the bygone age. That I have understood to be its meaning in Psalms and in Paul in the Epistle to Hebrews. In Psalms it is thus: "A thousand years are in thine eyes as a yesterday that had passed" (Psalm 90:4)—whatever the much talked of millennium means, it is likened to yesterday as opposed to today; and in the apostle it is written, "Jesus Christ is the same yesterday and today and unto the ages" (Hebrews 13:8). No wonder that the whole of an age counts with God as the space of a single day with us, aye and less as I think. We may also consider whether the accounts of feasts or assemblies recorded in terms of days or months or seasons or years have symbolical references to ages. For if the law contains a shadow of coming things, its many Sabbaths must be a shadow of many days and its moons come round in the course of intervals of time, completed by some manner of a moon's conjunction with some sun.

And if a first month and tenth till fourteenth day and a feast of unleavened bread from fourteenth till twenty-first contain a shadow of coming things, who is wise and to such a degree God's friend as to have vision of the first among many months and its tenth day and so on? What need I say of that feast of seven weeks of days, and of that seventh month whose new moon is a day of trumpets and on whose tenth day falls a day of atonement, which are known to God alone who has enacted them? Who has to such a degree received the mind of Christ as to interpret those seventh years of freedom for Hebrew domestic slaves and of remission of debts and of cessation from tillage of the holy land?

And over and above the feast of every seven years there is yet another year, the so-called Jubilee, clearly to imagine whose nature even partially, or the true laws to be fulfilled in it, is for no one save him who has contemplated the Father's counsel in reference to the order in all the ages, according to his unsearchable judgments and his uninvestigable ways. In trying to reconcile two apostolic passages, it has often occurred to me to raise the question how there can be consummation of ages at which Jesus has been manifested once for all unto abolition of sins if there are going to be ages following after this. The Apostles' passages are as follows: In the Epistle to Hebrews, "But now at a consummation of the ages he has been manifested once for all unto abolition of sins through his sacrifice" (Hebrews 9:26); but in the Epistle to Ephesians, "In order that he may show forth, in the years following, the exceeding riches of his grace in kindness toward us" (Ephesians 2:7).

Well, in conjecture as to matters so great, I believe that, just as the year's consummation is its last month after which arises another month's beginning, so probably the present age is a consummation of numerous ages, completing as it were a year of ages, and after it certain coming ages will arise whose beginning is the coming age, and in those coming ages God shall show forth the riches of his grace in kindness, when the greatest sinner, who for having spoken ill against the Holy Spirit is held fast by his sin throughout the present age and the coming one from beginning to end, shall after that, I know not how, receive a dispensation.

When a man has had vision of these things and has given thought to a week of ages with intent to contemplate a kind of holy sabbath-keeping, and a month of ages to see God's holy new moon, and a year of ages to survey the feasts of the year when every male must appear before the Lord God, and the corresponding years of so many ages to discern the seventh holy year, and seven weekly years of ages to sing a hymn to the Enactor of Laws so great, how can he after such consideration cavil over what is the merest fraction of an hour in the day of such an age, instead of doing everything to become, through his preparation here, worthy of obtaining the needful bread and to receive it while it is today and daily—what "daily" means being already clear from the foregoing explanations.

For he who prays today to God, who is from infinity to infinity, not only for today but also in a sense for that which is daily shall be enabled to receive from him who has power to bestow exceedingly above what we ask or think even things—to use extreme language—which transcend those that eye has not seen and ear has not heard and that have not gone up into the heart of man. These considerations seem to me to have been very necessary for the understanding of both the expressions today and daily when we are praying that the needful bread be given us from his Father.

CHAPTER 18

And forgive us our debts, as we also have forgiven our debtors

"And forgive us our debts, as we also have forgiven our debtors," or as Luke has it, "And forgive us our sins, for we also ourselves forgive everyone in debt to us." Concerning debts, the Apostle also says: "Pay your debts to all—to whom you owe tribute, tribute, to whom fear, fear, to whom taxes, taxes, to whom honor, honor: owe no man anything save mutual love" (Romans 13:7–8).

We owe therefore in having certain duties not only in giving but also in kind speech and corresponding actions, and indeed we owe a certain disposition towards one another. Owing these things, we either pay them through discharging the commands of the divine law, or failing to pay them, in contempt of the salutary word, we remain in debt. The like reflection applies to debts toward brothers, to those who in the religious sense have been born again with us in Christ, as well as to those who have a common mother or father with us.

We also have a certain debt toward fellow citizens, and another toward all men in common, in particular toward guests and toward men at the age of fatherhood, and another toward such as it is right that we should honor as sons or as brothers. He, therefore, who does not do what is a debt to be discharged to brothers remains a debtor for what he has not done. So, too, should we fail in what falls, at the prompting of the charitable spirit of wisdom, to human beings also at our hands, our indebtedness becomes the greater. Indeed, we also have debt in personal concerns—to use the body in a certain way, so as not to wear out the flesh of the body through love of pleasure, and on the other hand to treat the soul with a certain care, and to take forethought for the keenness of the mind, and for our speech that it be without sting and helpful and not trifling. Whenever we fail to perform what we owe, even to ourselves, the heavier does our debt become.

Besides all these, being above all a creation and formation of God, we owe it to preserve a certain disposition towards him with love that is from a whole heart and from a whole strength and from a whole mind, and if we fail to achieve this we remain God's debtors, sinning against the Lord. And who in that case shall pray for us? "For if a man sinning sin against a man, then shall they pray for him: but if he sin against the Lord, who shall pray for him?" as Eli says in the first book of Samuel (1 Samuel 2:25).

Moreover, we are debtors to Christ who bought us with his own blood, just as every house slave is also debtor to his purchaser for the sum of money given for him. We have also a certain indebtedness to the Holy Spirit: we are paying it when we do not grieve him in whom we were sealed unto a day of redemption, and when, without grieving him, we bear the fruits demanded of us, he being present with us and quickening our soul.

And even though we do not know precisely which is our individual angel that looks upon the face of the Father in heaven, it is at least manifest to each of us upon reflection that we are debtors to him also for certain things. And inasmuch as we are in a world theater both of angels and of men, one must know that as the performer in a theater owes it to say or do certain things in sight of the spectators, and if he fails to perform this is punished as having insulted the whole theater, so we, too, owe to the whole world, to all the angels and the race of men alike, those things which, if we have the will, we shall learn of wisdom.

Apart from those more general debts, there is a certain indebtedness to a widow who is being provided for by the church, a second to a deacon, another to an elder, while that to a bishop is heaviest of all—being demanded by the Savior of the whole church and avenged if not paid. As already said, the Apostle mentions a certain common debt between husband and wife, when he says: "Let the husband pay his indebtedness to the wife and wife likewise to the husband," and continues, "Deprive not one another" (1 Corinthians 7:3, 5).

But what need is there, when readers of this writing select their own examples from the record, for me to speak of all the things we owe which we either fail to pay and so come to be restrained, or else pay and come to be free? Suffice it to say that it is impossible while in this life to be without debt at any hour of night or day. In owing, a man either pays or else withholds the indebtedness. He may either pay or withhold in this life. Some indeed owe no man anything; others pay off most and owe little; others pay little and owe more; and a man may conceivably pay nothing and owe everything.

And besides, he who pays all so as to owe nothing may at sometimes effect his object if he prays for forgiveness for previous indebtedness, inasmuch as such forgiveness may reasonably be thought obtainable by one who has for sometime made it his ambition to reach the position of having no obligation unpaid and thus owing nothing. Our very activities in transgression leave their impression within our mind and become the indictment against us on which we shall be brought to trial when, as it were, the books that have been indicted by us all shall be brought forth, in the time when we shall all stand before the judgment seat of Christ that each may receive what he has earned through the body according to his conduct whether good or bad.

It is also in reference to such indebtedness that it is said in the Proverbs: "Give not yourself in certainty to your shame, for if the man shall not have ability to pay, they shall take your bed that is under you" (Proverbs 22:27). But if we owe to so many, it is certain that men owe to us also. Some owe to us as to human beings, others as to fellow citizens, others as to fathers, some as to sons, yet others as wives to husbands or as friends to friends. Whenever, accordingly, any of our very numerous debtors have behaved too remiss in the matter of payment of their dues to us, our more charitable course will be to bear them no grudge and to remember our own indebtedness and how often we have failed to discharge them not only towards men but also towards God himself.

Remembering what as debtors we have not paid but withheld during the time which it was our duty to have done this or that for our neighbor had run by, we shall be gentler toward those who have fallen in debt to us in turn and have not paid their indebtedness, especially if we do not forget our transgressions against the Divine and the unrighteousness we have spoken against the Height, either in ignorance of the truth or else in displeasure at the misfortunes that have befallen us.

But if we refuse to become gentler towards those who have fallen in debt to us, our experience will be that of him who did not remit the hundred pence to his fellow servant and of whom, according to the parable set down in the gospel, though already pardoned, the master exacts in severity what had already been remitted, saying to him: "Wicked servant and slothful, was it not right for you to pity your fellow servant as I also pitied you? Cast him into prison until he pay all that is owed." And the Lord continues: "So shall the heavenly Father do to you also if you forgive not each his brother from your hearts" (Matthew 18:32–34).

It is however on profession of penitence that we are to forgive those who have sinned against us, even though our debtor often does so; for he says: "If your brother sin against you seven times a day and seven times turn and say, 'I repent,' you shall forgive him" (Luke 17:4). It is not we who are harsh towards the impenitent, but they who are wicked to themselves, for he that spurns instruction hates himself. Yet even in such cases we should seek in every way that healing arise within him who is so completely perverted as not even to be conscious of his own ills but to be drunken with a drunkenness more fatal than from wine, from the darkening of evil.

When Luke says, "Forgive us our sins," he means the same as Matthew, since sins are constituted when we owe and do not pay, though he does not appear to lend support to him who would forgive only penitent debtors when he says that it is enacted by the Savior that we ought in prayer to add, "For we ourselves also forgive everyone in debt to us" (Luke 11:4). And it would seem that we have all authority to forgive the sins that have been committed against us as is clear from both clauses: "as we also have forgiven our debtors"; and "for we ourselves also forgive everyone in debt to us." But it is when a man is inspired by Jesus, as were the apostles, when he can be known from his fruits to have received the Spirit that is Holy and to have become spiritual through being led by the Spirit after the manner of a Son of God unto every reasonable duty, that he forgives whatsoever God has forgiven and holds those sins that are irremediable, and as the prophets served God in speaking not their own message but that of the divine will, so he too serves the God who alone has authority to forgive.

In the Gospel according to John, the language referring to the forgiveness exercised by the apostles runs thus: "Receive the Holy Spirit: whosoever's sins you forgive, they are forgiven unto them: whosoever's you hold, they are held" (John 20:22–23). Anyone taking these words without discrimination might blame the apostles for not forgiving all men in order that all might be forgiven but holding the sins of some so that they are held with God also on their account.

It is helpful to take an example from the Law with a view to understand God's forgiveness of sins through men. Legal priests are prohibited from offering sacrifice for certain sins, in order that the persons for whom the sacrifices are made may have their misdeeds forgiven; and though the priest has authority to make offerings for certain involuntary or willful misdeeds, he of course does not presume to offer a sacrifice for sin in cases of adultery or willful murder or any other more serious offence.

So, too, the apostles, and those who have become like apostles, being priests according to the Great High Priest and having received knowledge of the service of God, know under the Spirit's teaching for which sins, and when, and how they ought to offer sacrifices, and recognize for which they ought not to do so. Thus Eli the priest, knowing that his sons Hophni and Phinehas are sinners, with a sense of his inability to cooperate with them for forgiveness of sins, confesses his despair of such a result in his words: "If a man sins against a man, then shall they pray for him, but if he sin against the Lord, who shall pray for him?" (1 Samuel 2:25). I know not how it is, but there are some who have taken upon themselves what is beyond priestly dignity, perhaps through utter lack of accurate priestly knowledge, and are proud of their ability to pardon even acts of idolatry and to forgive acts of adultery and fornication, claiming that even sin unto death is absolved through their prayer for those who have dared to commit such.

They do not read the words, "There is sin unto death; not for it do I say that a man should ask" (1 John 5:16). Nor should we omit to mention the resolute Job's offering of sacrifice for his sons, with the words, "Perhaps my sons have had evil thoughts in their minds toward God" (Job 1:5). Though the sinful thoughts are doubtful and at worst have not reached the lips, he offers his sacrifice for them.

CHAPTER 19

And bring us not into temptation, but deliver us from evil

"And bring us not into temptation, but deliver us from evil." In Luke the words "but deliver us from evil" are omitted. Assuming that the Savior does not command us to pray for the impossible, it appears to me to deserve consideration in what sense we are bidden to pray not to enter into temptation, when all human life on earth is a test.

In that on earth we are beset by the flesh, which wars against the spirit and whose intent is enmity to God, as it is by no means capable of being subject to the law of God, we are in temptation. That all human life on earth is a trial we have learned from Job in the words, "Is not the life of men on earth a trial" (Job 7:1), and the same thing is made plain from the [eighteenth] psalm in the words, "In you will I be delivered from trial" (Psalm 18:30). Paul, too, writing to the Corinthians says that God bestows not freedom from temptation, but freedom from temptation beyond one's power.

More than human temptation has not possessed you, and God is to be trusted not to let you be tempted beyond your power, but to make the temptation be accompanied by the outlet of power to endure it. Whether our wrestling is with the flesh that lusts or wars against the spirit, or with the soul of all flesh—in other words the ruling faculty, called the heart, of the body in which it resides—as is the wrestling of those who are tempted with human temptations, or, as advanced and maturer athletes, who no longer wrestle with blood and flesh nor are reviewed in the human temptations which they have already trampled down, our struggles are with the principalities and authorities and world-rulers of his darkness and the Spiritual forces of evil, we have no release from temptation.

In what sense then does the Savior bid us pray not to enter into temptation, when God in some sense tempts all men? Think, says Judith, not only to the elders of that day but also to all readers of her writing, of all that he did with Abraham and all his temptations of Isaac and all that befell Jacob in Mesopotamia of Syria while he shepherded the flocks of Laban, his mother's brother (Judith 8:22–23). For it is not that whereas he tested them by fire for the proving of their hearts, the Lord who, for their admonishment, scourges those who approach him, now wreaks vengeance upon us.

And David declares as a general truth concerning all righteous men that "Many are the afflictions of the righteous" (Psalm 34:19), while in the Acts the Apostle says, "Because it is through many afflictions that we must enter into the kingdom of God" (Acts 14:21). And if we failed to understand what escapes most men in reference to prayer that we enter not into temptation, we would at this point say that the apostles were not heard in their prayers since throughout their whole time they endured countless sufferings: in toils more abundantly, in blows more abundantly, in prisons above measure, in deaths often, while Paul in particular five times received forty stripes save one at the hands of Jews, thrice was beaten with rods, once was stoned, thrice was shipwrecked, passed a night and a day in the deep—a man in every way afflicted, in straits, persecuted, cast down, confessing: "Until the present hour we have hungered, thirsted, gone naked, been buffeted, lacked rest, toiled at work with our own hands. Reviled, we have blessed; persecuted, we have borne up; slandered, we have exhorted (1 Corinthians 4:11–12).

When the apostles have failed in prayer, we might ask what hope there is for any of their inferiors to obtain God's hearing when one prays? One ignorant of the true meaning of the Savior's command will have reason to suppose that the words in the [twenty-sixth] psalm, "Test me, O Lord, and try me; assay my reins and my heart with fire" (Psalm 26:2), are in opposition to our Lord's teaching about prayer. And when has anyone ever believed that those of whom he had complete knowledge were free of temptations?

And what time can be conceived during which a man could be light-hearted as though he did not struggle to avoid sinning? Is a man poor? Let him beware lest one day he steal and forswear by the name of God. Again, is he rich? Let him not be lighthearted, for he may become completely false and say in exaltation, "Who sees me?" Even Paul, for all his riches, in all manner of discourse and in all manner of knowledge, is not released from the danger of sinning on their account through excessive exaltation, but needs a stake of Satan to buffet him in order that he may not be excessively exalted. Even though a man may have a comparatively good conscience and fly up in alarm from things evil, let him read what is said in the Second Book of Chronicles of Hezekiah, who is said to have fallen from the elevation of his heart.

And if, because I have not dwelt on the case of the poor, someone is lighthearted—as though poverty involved no temptation—he must know that the Plotter plots to cast down the needy and the poor, especially since according to Solomon, the needy endure no threats. And what need is there to tell how many, because of their material riches which they had failed to manage rightly, have found a place in punishment along with the rich man in the Gospel? And how many, because they bore poverty ignobly, with behavior more servile and base than was seemly in saints, have fallen away from their heavenly hope? Even they who are midway between these extremes of riches and poverty are not by any means released from sinning according to their possession, moderate though it be.

Again, one who is in bodily health and well-being imagines that by virtue of his mere health and well-being he is outside of all temptation. And yet, whose sin it is, apart from those in well being and in health, to corrupt the temple of God, no one will venture to say because the meaning of the passage is clear to everyone. And who in sickness has escaped the incitements to corrupt the temple of God, having leisure at such time and readily admitting thoughts of unclean things, not to speak of all the others things beside these which trouble him unless he guards his heart with all vigilance?

Many a man, overcome by troubles and incapable of bearing sickness manfully, has been shown to be suffering at the time from sickness rather of the soul than of the body, and many another, ashamed to bear the name of Christ nobly, has, through shunning disrepute, fallen into eternal shame. Again, a man may think that he has respite from temptation when he is in honor among men. Yet is not the Lord's saying, "They have their reward from men" (Matthew 6:2, 5), proclaimed to those who are elated over their popularity? Do not the words strike dismay: "How can you have come to believe, when you have received glory from one another, and seek not the glory which is from God alone" (John 5:44)?

And what need is there for me to recount the crimes done in pride by the reputed noble, and the fawning submission of the so-called low-born towards the reputed noble by reason of their ignorance, a submission which separates from God men who are devoid of genuine friendliness but feign that fairest of human possessions—love. The whole life of man on earth is therefore a trial, as has already been said. Let us for that reason pray for deliverance from trial, not through being exempt from it—that is an utter impossibility for beings on earth—but through not succumbing under it.

It is when a man succumbs in the moment of tempting, I take it, that he enters into temptation, being held in its nets. Into those nets the Savior entered for the sake of those who had already been caught in them, and in the words of the Song of Songs, looking out through the meshwork makes answer to those who have been already caught by them and have entered into temptation, and says to those who form his bride, "Arise, my dear one, my fair one, my dove" (Song of Songs 2:10). To bring home the fact that every time is one of temptation on earth, I will add that even he who meditates upon the law of God day and night and makes a practice of carrying out the saying, "A righteous man's mouth shall meditate on wisdom" (Psalm 37:30), has no release from being tempted. How many in their devotion to the examination of the divine Scriptures have, through misunderstanding the messages contained in Law and Prophets, devoted themselves to godless and impious or to foolish and ridiculous opinions?

What need is there for me to answer, when there are countless examples of such mistakes among those who do not seem to be open to the charge of righteousness in their reading? The same fate has also overtaken many in their reading of the Apostles and Gospels inasmuch as, through their own lack of discernment, they fashion in imagination a Son or a Father other than the One divinely conceived and truly recognized by Holy Writ. For one who fails to have true thoughts of God or his Christ has fallen away from the true God and from his Only Begotten, and his worship of the imaginary Father and Son, fashioned by his lack of discernment, is no real worship. Such is his fate through having failed to recognize the temptation present in the reading of Holy Writ to arm himself and take a stand as for a struggle already upon him.

We ought therefore to pray, not that we be not tempted—that is impossible—but that we be not encompassed by temptation, the fate of those who are open to it and are overcome. Now since, outside of the Lord's Prayer, it is written "Pray that you enter not into temptation"

(Matthew 26:41), the force of which may perhaps be clear from what has already been said, whereas in the Lord's Prayer we ought to say to God our Father, "Bring us not into Temptation," it is worth seeing in what sense we ought to think of God as leading one who does not pray or is not heard into temptation. If entering into temptation means being overcome, it is manifestly out of the question to think that God leads anyone into temptation, as though he delivered him to be overcome.

The same difficulty awaits one no matter in what sense one may interpret the words "Pray that you enter not into temptation," for if it is an evil to fall into temptation, which we pray may not be our fate, must it not be out of place to think of the Good God, who is incapable of bearing evil fruits, as encompassing anyone with evils? It is of service to cite in this connection what Paul has said in the Epistle to Romans—thus: "Claiming to be wise they became foolish and changed the glory of the incorruptible God into the likeness of an image of corruptible man and of winged and four footed and creeping things. Wherefore God delivered them in the lusts of their hearts unto uncleanness to the dishonoring of their bodies among themselves" (Romans 1:23–24); and shortly after: "Therefore God delivered them unto passions of dishonor: for both their females changed the natural use into the unnatural, and the males likewise setting aside the natural use of the female, were consumed," and so on (Romans 1:26–27). And again shortly after: "And as they proved not to have God in full knowledge, God delivered them unto a reprobate mind to do the unseemly" (Romans 1:28).

We may simply confront dividers of the Godhead with all these passages and put these questions to them, since they hold that the good Father of Our Lord is distinct from the God of the law. Is it the good God who leads into temptation one who fails in prayer? Is it the Father of the Lord who delivers in the lusts of their hearts those who have already done some sin unto uncleanness to the dishonoring of their bodies among themselves? Is it he who, as they themselves say, is free from judging and punishing, who delivers unto passions of dishonor and unto a reprobate mind to do the unseemly men who would not have fallen into the lusts of their hearts had they not been delivered to them by God, who would not have succumbed to passions of dishonor had they not been delivered to them by God, and who would not have lapsed into a reprobate mind but for the fact that the so condemned had been delivered to it by God.

I am well aware that these passages will trouble such thinkers exceedingly. Indeed they have fashioned in imagination a God other than the Maker of heaven and earth, because they find many such passages in the Law and the Prophets and have been offended by the author of such utterances as not good. But I on my part, for the sake of that question, raised in connection with the words "Bring us not into Temptation," which led to my citation of the apostle's words also, must now consider whether I in turn find a solution of apparent contradictions worth considering. Well, it is my belief that God rules over each rational soul, having regard to its everlasting life, in such a way that it is always in possession of free will and is itself responsible alike for being, in the better way, in progress towards the perfection of goodness, or otherwise for descending as the result of heedlessness to this or that degree of aggravation of vice.

Accordingly, since a swift and somewhat short cure gives rise in some men to a contempt for the disease into which they have fallen, with the possible result of their incurring it a second time, he will in such other cases with good reason allow the vice to increase to a certain extent, suffering it even to be aggravated in them to the verge of incurableness, in order that they may be sated through long continuance in the evil and through surfeit of the sin for which they lust, and may be brought to a sense of their injury, and, having learned to hate what formerly they welcomed, may be enabled when cured to enjoy more steadfastly the health which their cure has brought to their souls. So it was that the mixed throng among the children of Israel, once fell into lust.

Sitting down, they and the children of Israel cried out saying, "Who will give us flesh to eat? We remember the fish we used to eat freely in Egypt, and the cucumbers and melons and leeks and onions and garlic, but now is our soul parched; our eyes are on nothing save the manna" (Numbers 11:4–6). Then, shortly after, it is said: "And Moses heard them crying in their tribes; each was at his door" (Numbers 11:10). And again shortly after the Lord says to Moses: And you shall say to the people, "Sanctify yourselves for the morrow, and eat flesh, because you have cried before the Lord saying, 'Who will give us flesh to eat, because it was well with us in Egypt,' and the Lord shall give you flesh to eat. So eat flesh! Eat it not one nor two nor five days, not ten nor twenty days; for a month of days eat till it issue from your nostrils, and it shall make you ill, because you have disobeyed the Lord who is among you, and have cried before him, 'Wherefore have we left Egypt?'" (Numbers 11:18–20). Let us therefore see whether the narrative I have laid before you as a parallel is of help towards a solution of the apparent contradiction in the clause "Bring us not into temptation" and in the words of the apostle. Having fallen into lust, the mixed throng among the children of Israel cried and the children of Israel with them.

Plainly so long as they were without the objects of their lust, they were not able to be sated with them or cease their passion. In fact, it was the will of the benevolent and good God, in giving them the object of their lust, not to give it in such a way that any lust should be left in them. For that reason he tells them to eat the flesh not one day—for had they partaken of the flesh a short time, their passion would have remained in their soul, which would have been kindled and set ablaze by it—nor does he give them the object of their lust for two days.

It being his will to make it excessive for them, he utters what is, to one who can understand, a threat rather than a promise of their apparent gratification, saying: "Neither shall you pass five days eating the flesh nor twofold those, nor yet twofold those again, but eat flesh for a whole mouth, until such time as your imagined good shall issue from your nostrils with choleric affection, and with it your culpable and base lust for it. So shall I set you free from all further lust of living, that when you have come out in such condition, you may be pure from lust and may remember all the troubles through which you were set free from it. Thus you shall be enabled either not to fall into it again, or, should that ever happen through forgetfulness during the long lapse of time of your sufferings on account of lust, if you take no heed to yourselves and not appropriate the Word that completely frees you from every passion, if you fall into evil and at a later time, through having come to lust again for creation, require a second time to obtain the objects of your lust—in hatred of that object revert again to the good and heavenly nourishment through despising that which you longed for the most."

The like fate, accordingly, will overtake those who have changed the glory of the incorruptible God into the likeness of an image of corruptible man and of winged and four-footed and creeping things, and who are forsaken of God and thereby delivered in the lusts of their hearts unto uncleanness to the dishonoring of their bodies, as men who have brought down to soulless insensible matter the name of him who has bestowed upon all sentient rational beings not only sense but even rational sense, and to some indeed a complete and excellent sense and intelligence. Such men are reasonably delivered to passion of dishonor by the God whom they have forsaken, being forsaken by him in return, receiving the requital of error through which they came to love the itch for pleasure.

For it is more of a requital of their error for them to be delivered to passions of dishonor than to be cleansed by the fire of Wisdom and to have each of their debts exacted from them in prison to the last farthing. For in being delivered to passions of dishonor which are not only natural but many of the unnatural, they are debased and hardened by the flesh and become as though they had no soul or intelligence any longer but were flesh entirely; whereas in fire and prison they receive not requital of their error but benefaction for the cleansing of the evil contracted in their error, along with salutary sufferings attendant in the pleasure-loving and are thereby set free from all stain and blood in whose defilement and pollution they had to their own undoing been unable even to think of being saved.

So their God shall wash away the stain of the sons and daughters of Zion and shall cleanse away the blood from their midst with a spirit of judgment and a spirit of burning: for he comes in as the fire of a furnace and as soap, washing and cleansing those who are in need of such remedies because it has not been their clear desire to have knowledge of God. After being delivered to these remedies they will of their own accord hate the reprobate mind, for it is God's will that a man acquire goodness not as under necessity but of his own accord. Some, it may well be, will have had difficulty in perceiving the baseness of evil as the result of long familiarity with it, but then turning away from it as falsely taken to be good.

Consider, too, whether God's reason for hardening the heart of Pharaoh also is that he may, because hardened, be unable to say, as in fact he did, "The Lord is righteous, but I and my people are impious." Rather it is that he needs more and more to be hardened and to undergo certain sufferings, in order that he may not, as the result of a too speedy end to the hardening, despise hardening as an evil and frequently again deserve to be hardened.

If their nets are not wrongfully stretched for birds, according to the statement in the Proverbs, but God rightly leads men into the snare, as one has said, "You led us into the snare," and if not even a sparrow, cheapest of birds, falls into the snare without the counsel of the Father, its fall into the snare being due to the failure to use aright its control of its wings given to it to soar, let us pray to do nothing to deserve being brought into temptation by the righteous judgment of God, as in the case with everyone who is delivered by God in the lusts of his own heart unto uncleanness, or delivered unto passions of dishonor, or as not having proved to have God in full knowledge, is delivered unto a reprobate mind to do the unseemly. The use of temptation is somewhat as follows. Through temptations, the content of our soul, which is a secret to all except God, ourselves included, becomes manifest, in order that it may no longer be a secret to us what manner of men we are, but that we may have fuller knowledge of ourselves and realize, if we choose, our own evils and be thankful for the blessings manifested to us through temptations. That the temptations which befall us take place for the revealing of our true nature or the discerning of what is hidden in our heart, is set forth by the Lord's saying in Job and by the scripture in Deuteronomy, which runs thus: "Do you think that I have uttered speech to you for any reason other than that you may be revealed as righteous?" (Job 40:8). And in Deuteronomy: "He afflicted you and starved you and gave you manna to eat, and he led you about in the wilderness where biting serpents and scorpions and thirst are, that the things in your heart might be discerned" (Deuteronomy 8:15–16). And if we desire references to plain history, it is matter of knowledge that Eve's readiness to be deceived and unsoundness of thought did not originate when in disobedience to God she hearkened to the serpent, but had already been betrayed, the reason for the serpent's having engaged her being that with its peculiar wisdom it had perceived her weakness.

Nor was it the beginning of evil in Cain where he slew his brother, for already the heart-knowing God had little regard for Cain and his sacrifices. It was simply that his wickedness became manifest when he took Abel's life. Had Noah not drunk of the wine that he cultivated and become intoxicated and uncovered himself, neither Ham's indiscretion and irreverence towards his father nor his brother's reverence and modesty towards their parent would have been revealed.

Though Esau's plot against Jacob seemed to have provided an excuse for his being deprived of the blessing, his soul even before that had roots of fornication and profanity. And we should never have known of the splendor of Joseph's self-control, prepared as he was against falling a victim to any lust, had his master's wife not fallen in love with him. Let us therefore, in the intervals between the succession of temptations, make a stand against the impending trial, and prepare ourselves for all possible contingencies—in order that, come what may, we may not be convicted of unreadiness but may be shown to have braced ourselves with the utmost care. For when we have carried out all our part, the deficiency caused by human weakness will be filled up by God who cooperates for good in all things with those who love him, and whose future growth has been foreseen according to his unerring knowledge.

In the words "Bring us not into temptation," Luke seems to me to have virtually taught "Deliver us from evil" also. In any case it is natural that the Lord should have addressed the briefer form to the disciple as he had already been helped, but the more explicit to the many who were in need of clearer teaching. God delivers us from evil, not when the enemy does not engage us at all in conflict through any of his own wiles or those of the ministers of his will, but when we make a manful stand against contingencies and are victorious.

In that sense I have also taken the words: "Many are the afflictions of the righteous: and he delivers them from them all" (Psalm 34:19). For God delivers us from afflictions not when afflictions are no more—and surely Paul's expression "in everything afflicted" (2 Corinthians 4:8) implies that affliction had never yet ceased—but when, by God's help, under affliction we are not straitened.

According to a usage native to Hebrews, "affliction" denotes misfortune that happens without reference to a human will, whereas "straitening" refers to the will overcome by affliction and surrendered to it. Hence Paul well says, "in everything afflicted but not impoverished." And I consider the words in Psalms "In affliction you set me at large" to be similar, for by "setting at large" is meant the joyousness and cheerfulness of temper which comes to us from God in the season of misfortune through the cooperation and presence of God's encouraging and saving Word. We are accordingly to understand deliverance from evil in the same way. God delivered Job, not through the Devil's failure to receive authority to beset him with certain temptations—for he did receive it—but through his own avoidance of sin in the sight of God amidst all that befell him and through the exhibition of his righteousness.

Thus he who had said, "Does Job revere God for nothing? Have you not fenced about with a circle his goods without and his goods within the house and the goods of all who are his, and blessed his work and made his flocks and herds to abound on the earth? But send forth your hand, and touch all that he has, and surely he will curse you to your face" (Job 1:9–11) was put to shame as having thereby spoken falsely against Job, for he, after all his suffering, did not, as the Adversary said, curse God to his face, but even when delivered to the tempter he continued steadfastly blessing God, reproving his wife for saying, "Speak some word against God and die" (Job 2:9), and rebuking her in the words: "As one of the senseless women have you spoken" (Job 2:10).

If we have accepted the good from the Lord's hand, shall we not endure the evil? And a second time concerning Job, the Devil said to the Lord: "Skin for skin; all that the man has he will pay for his soul. Nay but send forth your hand and touch his bones and his flesh, and surely he will curse you to your face" (Job 2:4–5). But he is overcome by the champion of virtue and shown to be a liar, for Job in spite of the severest sufferings stood firm committing no sin with his lips in the sight of God. Two falls did Job wrestle and conquer, but no third such struggle did he undergo, for the threefold wrestling had to be reserved for the Savior, as it is recorded in the three Gospels, when the Savior known in human form thrice conquered the Enemy. In order therefore to ask of God intelligently that we enter not into temptation and that we be delivered from evil, let us consider these things and investigate them in our own minds more carefully. Through hearkening unto God, let us become worthy to be heard by him, and let our entreaty be that when tempted we may not be brought to death, and that when assailed by flaming darts of evil, we may not be set on fire by them.

All whose hearts are (as one of the Twelve Prophets says, as an ember-pan) are set on fire by them, but not so they who with the shield of faith quench all the flaming darts aimed at them by the Evil One, since they have within themselves rivers of water springing up into life eternal which do not let the fire of the Evil One prevail but readily undo it with the flood of their inspired and saving thought that is impressed by contemplation of the truth upon the soul of him whose study is to be spiritual.

CHAPTER 20

Formalities of prayer: Conclusion

I think it not out of place to add, by way of completing my task in reference to prayer, a somewhat elementary discussion of such matters as the disposition and the posture that is right for one who prays, the place where one ought to pray, the direction towards which one ought except in any special circumstances to look, and the time suitable and marked out for prayer.

The seat of disposition is to be found in the soul, that of the posture in the body. Thus Paul, as we observed above, suggests the disposition in speaking of the duty of praying without anger and disputation and the posture in the words lifting up holy hands, which he seems to me to have taken from the Psalms where it stands thus: "the lifting up of my hands as evening sacrifice" (Psalm 140:2); as to the place, "I desire therefore that men pray in every place" (1 Timothy 2:8); and as to the direction in the Wisdom of Solomon: "that it might be known that it is right to go before the sun to give thanks to you and to intercede with you towards the dawn of light" (Wisdom 16:28).

Accordingly it seems to me that one who is about to enter upon prayer ought first to have paused awhile and prepared himself to engage in prayer throughout more earnestly and intently, to have cast aside every distraction and confusion of thought, to have bethought him to the best of his ability of the greatness of him whom he is approaching and of the impiety of approaching him frivolously and carelessly and, as it were, in contempt, and to have put away everything alien.

He ought thus to enter upon prayer with his soul, as it were, extended before his hands, and his mind intent on God before his eyes, and his intellect raised from earth and set toward the Lord of All before his body stands. Let him put away all resentment against any real or imagined injurer in proportion to his desire for God not to bear resentment against himself in turn for his injuries and sins against many of his neighbors or any wrong deeds whatsoever upon his conscience.

Of all the innumerable dispositions of the body that, accompanied by outstretching of the hands and upraising of the eyes, standing is preferred—inasmuch as one thereby wears in the body also the image of the devotional characteristics that become the soul. I say that these things ought to be observed by preference except in any special circumstances, for in special circumstances, by reason of some serious foot disease one may upon occasion quite properly pray sitting, or by reason of fevers or similar illnesses, lying, and indeed owing to circumstances, if, let us say, we are on a voyage or if our business does not permit us to retire to pay our debt of prayer, we may pray without any outward sign of doing so.

Moreover, one must know that kneeling is necessary when he is about to arraign his personal sins against God with supplication for their healing and forgiveness, because it is a symbol of submission and subjection. For Paul says: "For this cause I bow my knees unto the Father from whom is all fatherhood named in heaven and on earth" (Ephesians 3:14–15). It may be termed spiritual kneeling, because of the submission and self-humiliation of every being to God in the name of Jesus, that the apostle appears to indicate in the words: "that in the name of Jesus every knee should bow in heaven and on earth and under the earth" (Philippians 2:10).

It should not be supposed that beings in heaven have bodies so fashioned as actually to possess knees, since their bodies have been described possibly as spherical in form by those who have discussed these matters more minutely. He who refuses to admit this will also, unless he outrages reason, admit the uses of each of the members in order that nothing fashioned for them by God may be in vain. One falls into error on either hand, whether he shall assert that bodily members have been brought into being by God for them in vain and not for their proper work, or shall say that the internal organs, the intestine included, perform their proper uses even in heavenly beings. Exceedingly foolish will it be to think that it is only their surface, as with statues, that is human in form and nothing further underneath.

This much discussion will suffice, then, of kneeling and of seeing that,

"In the name of Jesus every knee shall bow in heaven and on earth and under the earth." To the same effect, it is written by the prophet, "To me every knee shall bow." In regard to place, it should be known that, "Every place is rendered fit for prayer by one who prays rightly, for in every place sacrifice is offered to me . . . says the Lord, and I desire therefore that men pray in every place."

But to secure the performance of one's prayers in peace without distraction, the rule is for every man to make choice, if possible, of what I may term the most solemn spot in his house before he prays, considering in addition to his general examination of it, whether any violation of law or right has not been done in the place in which he is praying, so as to have made not only himself but also the place of his personal prayer of such a nature that the regard of God has fled from it.

And in reference to this matter of place, lengthy consideration leads me to say what may seem to be harsh, but what, if one inquires into it carefully, may possibly not invite contempt, namely that it is a question whether it is reverent and pure to intercede with God in the place of that union which is not unlawful but is conceded by the Apostle's word by way of indulgence not injunction. For if it is not possible to give oneself to prayer as one ought without devoting oneself to it by agreement for a season, the matter of the place also may possibly deserve to be considered if possible.

Yet there is a certain helpful charm in a place of prayer being the spot in which believers meet together. Also it may well be that the assemblies of believers also are attended by angelic powers, by the powers of our Lord and Savior himself, and indeed by the spirits of saints, including those already fallen asleep, certainly of those still in life, though just how is not easy to say. In reference to angels we may reason thus. If an angel of the Lord shall encamp round about those that fear him and shall deliver them, and if Jacob's words are true, not only of himself but to all who have devoted themselves to God, when we understand him to say the angel who delivers me from all evil, it is natural to infer that, when a number of men are genuinely met for Christ's glory, that angel of each man—who is round about each of those that fear—will encamp with the man with whose guardianship and stewardship he has been entrusted, so that when saints assemble together there is a twofold church, the one of men the other of angels.

And although it is only the prayer of Tobit, and after him of Sarah who later became his daughter-in-law owing to her marriage to Tobias, that Raphael says he has offered up as a memorial, what happens when several are linked in one mind and conviction and are formed into one body in Christ? In reference to the presence of the power of the Lord with the church Paul says, "You being gathered together with my spirit and with the power of the Lord Jesus" (1 Corinthians 5:4), implying that the Lord Jesus' power is not only with the Ephesians but also with the Corinthians.

And if Paul, while still wearing the body, believed that he assisted in Corinth with his spirit, we need not abandon the belief that the blessed departed in spirit also, perhaps more than one who is in the body, make their way likewise into the churches. For that reason we ought not to despise prayer in churches, recognizing that it possesses a special virtue for him who genuinely joins in.

And just as Jesus' power and the spirit of Paul and similar men, and the angels of the Lord who encamp round about each of the saints, are associated and join with those who genuinely assemble themselves together, so we may conjecture that if any man be unworthy of a holy angel and give himself up through sin and transgressions in contempt of God to a devil's angel, he will perhaps, in the event of those like him being few, not long escape that providence of those angels which oversee the church by the authority of the divine will and will bring the misdeeds of such persons to general knowledge; whereas if such persons become numerous and meet as mere human societies with business of the more material sort, they will not be overseen.

That is shown in Isaiah when the Lord says: "Neither if you shall come to appear before me; for I will turn away my eyes from you, and even if you multiply your supplication I will not pay attention" (Isaiah 1:15).

For in place of the already mentioned twofold company of saintly men and blessed angels there may, on the other hand, be a twofold association of impious men and evil angels. Of such a congregation it might be said alike by holy angels and by pious men: "I sat not down with the council of vanity, and with transgressors I will not enter in; I hated the church of evildoers and with the impious I will not sit down" (Psalm 25:4–5). I think that it was also for such a reason that the people in Jerusalem and the whole of Judea, having come to be in a state of great sinfulness, became subject to their enemies through the abandonment by God and the overshielding angels and the saving work of saintly men—having become people who have abandoned the Law.

For whole gatherings are at times thus abandoned to fall into temptation in order that even that which they seem to have may be taken away from them. Like the fig tree that was cursed and taken away from the roots because it had not given fruit to the hungering Jesus, they wither and lose any little amount they once had of lively power according to faith.

So much for what seem to me to have been necessary observations in considering the place of prayer and in setting forth its special virtue in respect to place in the case of the meetings of saintly men who come together reverently in churches. A few words may now be added in reference to the direction in which one ought to look in prayer. Of the four directions, the North, South, East, and West, who would not at once admit that the East clearly indicates the duty of praying with the face turned towards it with the symbolic suggestion that the soul is looking upon the dawn of the true light?

Should anyone, however, prefer to direct his intercessions according to the aperture of the house, whichever way the doors of the house may face, saying that the sight of heaven appeals to one with a certain attraction greater than the view of the wall, and the eastward part of the house having no opening, we may say to him that since it is by human arrangement that houses are open in this or that direction but by nature that the East is preferred to all the other directions, the natural is to be set before the artificial. Besides, on that view why should one who wished to pray when in the open country pray to the East in preference to the

West? If, in the one case it is reasonable to prefer the East, why should the same not be done in every case? Enough on that subject.

I have still to treat the topics of prayer, and therewith I purpose to bring this treatise to an end. Four topics which I have found scattered throughout the Scriptures appear to me to deserve mention, and according to these everyone should organize their prayer. The topics are as follows.

In the beginning and opening of prayer, glory is to be ascribed according to one's ability to God, through Christ who is to be glorified with him, and in the Holy Spirit who is to be proclaimed with him.

Thereafter, one should put thanksgivings: common thanksgivings— into which he introduces benefits conferred upon men in general—and thanksgivings for things which he has personally received from God. After thanksgiving, it appears to me that one ought to become a powerful accuser of one's own sins before God and ask first for healing with a view to being released from the habit which brings on sin, and secondly for forgiveness for past actions. After confession it appears to me that one ought to append, as a fourth element, the asking for the great and heavenly things, both personal and general, on behalf of one's nearest and dearest. And last of all, one should bring prayer to an end ascribing glory to God through Jesus Christ in the Holy Spirit. As I already said, I have found these points scattered throughout the scriptures.

The element of glorious ascription occurs in these words in the one hundred and [fourth] psalm: "O Lord, my God, how exceedingly you are magnified. You have put on praise and majesty, who are he that wraps himself in light as in a mantel, who stretches out the heaven like a curtain, who roofs his upper chambers with waters, who makes clouds his chariot, who walks on wings of winds, who makes winds his angels and flaming fire his ministers, who lays the foundations of the earth for its safety—it shall not swerve for ever and ever; the deep is a mantle of his vestment; on the mountains shall waters stand; from your rebuke shall they flee; from the sound of your thunder shall they shrink in fear" (Psalm 104:1–7).

Indeed most of the psalm contains ascription of glory to the Father. But anyone may select numerous passages for himself and see how broadly the element of glorious ascription is scattered. Of thanksgiving, this may be set forth as an example. It is found in the second book of Samuel, and is uttered by David, after promises made through Nathan to David, in astonishment at the bounties of God and in thanksgiving for them. It runs: "Who am I, O Lord my Lord, and what is my house, that you have loved me to this extent? I am exceeding small in your sight, my Lord, and yet you have spoken on behalf of the house of your servant for a long time to come. Such is the way of man, O Lord my Lord, and what shall David go on to say more to you? Even now you know your servant, O Lord. For your servant have you wrought and according to your heart have you wrought all this greatness to make it known to your servant that he should magnify you, O Lord my Lord" (2 Samuel 7:18–22).

Of confessions we have an example in "From all my transgressions deliver me" (Psalm 39:9). And elsewhere: "My wounds have stunk and been corrupt because of my folly. I have been wretched and bowed down utterly; all the day have I gone with sullen face" (Psalm 38:6–7). Of petitions we have an example in the [twenty-eighth] psalm: "Draw me not away with sinners, and destroy me not with workers of unrighteousness," and the like (Psalm 28:3). And it is right as one began with ascription of glory, to bring one's prayers to an end in ascription of glory, singing and glorifying the Father of all through Jesus Christ in the Holy Spirit—to whom be glory unto eternity.

Thus, Ambrosius and Tatiana, studious and genuine brethren in piety, according to my ability I have struggled through my treatment of the subject of prayer and of the prayer in the Gospels together with its preface in Matthew. But if you press on to the things in front and forget those behind and pray for me in my undertaking, I do not despair of being enabled to receive from God the Giver a fuller and more divine capacity for all these matters, and with it to discuss the same subject again in a nobler, loftier, and clearer way. Meanwhile, however, you will peruse this with indulgence.

Cassian

The First Conference of Abbot Isaac

On Prayer

CHAPTER 1

Introduction to the conference

What was promised in the second book of the *Institutes* on continual and unceasing perseverance in prayer shall be, by the Lord's help, fulfilled by the Conferences of this Elder, whom we will now bring forward, viz., Abbot Isaac. And when these have been propounded, I think that I shall have satisfied the commands of Pope Castor, of blessed memory, and your wishes, O blessed Pope Leontius and holy brother Helladius, and the length of the book in its earlier part may be excused, though, in spite of our endeavor not only to compress what had to be told into a brief discourse, but also to pass over very many points in silence, it has been extended to a greater length than we intended. For having commenced with a full discourse on various regulations, which we have thought it well to curtail for the sake of brevity, at the close the blessed Isaac spoke these words.

CHAPTER 2

The words of Abbot Isaac on the nature of prayer

The aim of every monk and the perfection of his heart tends to continual
and unbroken perseverance in prayer, and, as far as it is allowed to human
frailty, strives to acquire an immovable tranquillity of mind and a perpetual purity, for the sake of which we seek unweariedly and constantly
to practice all bodily labors, as well as contrition of spirit.

And there is between these two a sort of reciprocal and inseparable
union. For just as the crown of the building of all virtues is the perfection
of prayer, so unless everything has been united and compacted by this
as its crown, it cannot possibly continue strong and stable. For lasting
and continual calmness in prayer, of which we are speaking, cannot be
secured or consummated without them; so neither can those virtues
which lay its foundations be fully gained without persistence in it. And
so we shall not be able either to treat properly of the effect of prayer, or
in a rapid discourse to penetrate to its main end, which is acquired by
laboring at all virtues, unless first all those things which for its sake must
be either rejected or secured are singly enumerated and discussed, and,
as the parable in the gospel teaches (Luke 14:28), whatever concerns the
building of that spiritual and most lofty tower is reckoned up and carefully considered beforehand.

But yet these things when prepared will be of no use nor allow the
lofty height of perfection to be properly placed upon them unless a clear-
ance of all faults be first undertaken, and the decayed and dead rubbish
of the passions be dug up, and the strong foundations of simplicity and
humility be laid on the solid and (so to speak) living soil of our breast, or
rather on that rock of the gospel (Luke 6:48), and by being built in this
way this tower of spiritual virtues will rise, and be able to stand unmoved,
and be raised to the utmost heights of heaven in full assurance of its
stability. For if it rests on such foundations, then though heavy storms
of passions break over it, though mighty torrents of persecutions beat
against it like a battering ram, though a furious tempest of spiritual foes

dash against it and attack it, yet not only will no ruin overtake it, but the onslaught will not injure it even in the slightest degree.

CHAPTER 3
How pure and sincere prayer can be gained

And therefore in order that prayer may be offered up with that earnestness and purity with which it ought to be, we must by all means observe these rules.

First, all anxiety about carnal things must be entirely got rid of; next, we must leave no room for not merely the care but even the recollection of any business affairs; and in like manner also must lay aside all backbitings, vain and incessant chattering, and buffoonery. Anger above all and disturbing moroseness must be entirely destroyed, and the deadly taint of carnal lust and covetousness be torn up by the roots.

And so when these and such like faults which are also visible to the eyes of men, are entirely removed and cut off, and when such a purification and cleansing, as we spoke of, has first taken place—which is brought about by pure simplicity and innocence—then first there must be laid the secure foundations of a deep humility, which may be able to support a tower that shall reach the sky; and next the spiritual structure of the virtues must be built up upon them, and the soul kept free from all conversation and from roving thoughts, that thus it may by little and little begin to rise to the contemplation of God and to spiritual insight. For whatever our mind has been thinking of before the hour of prayer is sure to occur to us while we are praying through the activity of the memory.

Wherefore what we want to find ourselves like while we are praying, that we ought to prepare ourselves to be before the time for prayer. For the mind in prayer is formed by its previous condition, and when we are applying ourselves to prayer the images of the same actions and words and thoughts will dance before our eyes, and make us either angry, as in our previous condition, or gloomy, or recall our former lust and business, or make us shake with foolish laughter (which I am ashamed to speak of) at some silly joke, or smile at some action, or fly back to our previous conversation. And therefore if we do not want anything to haunt us while we are praying, we should be careful before our prayer, to exclude it from the shrine of our heart, that we may thus fulfill the Apostle's injunction: "Pray without ceasing" (1 Thessalonians 5:17), and, "In every place lifting up holy hands without wrath or disputing" (1 Timothy 2:8). For otherwise we shall not be able to carry out that charge unless our mind, purified from all stains of sin, and given over to virtue as to its natural good, feed on the continual contemplation of Almighty God.

CHAPTER 4

Of the lightness of the soul which may be compared to a wing or feather

For the nature of the soul is not inaptly compared to a very fine feather or very light wing, which, if it has not been damaged or affected by being spoilt by any moisture falling on it from without, is borne aloft almost naturally to the heights of heaven by the lightness of its nature and the aid of the slightest breath. But if it is weighted by any moisture falling upon it and penetrating into it, it will not only not be carried away by its natural lightness into any aerial flights, but will actually be borne down to the depths of earth by the weight of the moisture it has received.

So also our soul, if it is not weighted with faults that touch it, and the cares of this world, or damaged by the moisture of injurious lusts, will be raised as it were by the natural blessing of its own purity and borne aloft to the heights by the light breath of spiritual meditation; and leaving things low and earthly will be transported to those that are heavenly and invisible. Wherefore we are well warned by the Lord's command, "Take heed that your hearts be not weighed down by surfeiting and drunkenness and the cares of this world" (Luke 21:34). And therefore if we want our prayers to reach not only the sky, but what is beyond the sky, let us be careful to reduce our soul, purged from all earthly faults and purified from every stain, to its natural lightness, that so our prayer may rise to God unchecked by the weight of any sin.

CHAPTER 5
Of the ways in which our soul is weighed down

But we should notice the ways in which the Lord points out that the soul is weighed down: for he did not mention adultery, or fornication, or murder, or blasphemy, or rapine, which everybody knows to be deadly and damnable, but surfeiting and drunkenness, and the cares or anxieties of this world: which men of this world are so far from avoiding or considering damnable that actually some who (I am ashamed to say) call themselves monks entangle themselves in these very occupations as if they were harmless or useful. And though these three things, when literally given way to weigh down the soul, and separate it from God, and bear it down to things earthly, yet it is very easy to avoid them, especially for us who are separated by so great a distance from all converse with this world, and who do not on any occasion have anything to do with those visible cares and drunkenness and surfeiting.

But there is another surfeiting which is no less dangerous, and a spiritual drunkenness which it is harder to avoid, and a care and anxiety of this world, which often ensnares us even after the perfect renunciation of all our goods, and abstinence from wine and all feastings and even when we are living in solitude—and of such the prophet says, "Awake, you that are drunk but not with wine" (Joel 1:5), and another, "Be astonished and wonder and stagger: be drunk and not with wine: be moved, but not with drunkenness" (Isaiah 29:9). And of this drunkenness the wine must consequently be what the prophet calls "the fury of dragons." And from what root the wine comes you may hear: "From the vineyard of Sodom," he says, "is their vine, and their branches from Gomorrha." Would you also know about the fruit of that vine and the seed of that branch? "Their grape is a grape of gall, theirs is a cluster of bitterness"

(Deuteronomy 32:32–33). For unless we are altogether cleansed from all faults and abstaining from the surfeit of all passions, our heart will without drunkenness from wine and excess of any feasting be weighed down by a drunkenness and surfeiting that is still more dangerous. For that worldly cares can sometimes fall on us who mix with no actions of this world, is clearly shown according to the rule of the Elders, who have laid down that anything which goes beyond the necessities of daily food, and the unavoidable needs of the flesh, belongs to worldly cares and anxieties, as for example if, when a job bringing in a penny would satisfy the needs of our body, we try to extend it by a longer toil and work in order to get twopence or threepence; and when a covering of two tunics would be enough for our use both by night and day, we manage to become the owners of three or four, or when a hut containing one or two cells would be sufficient, in the pride of worldly ambition and greatness we build four or five cells, and these splendidly decorated, and larger than our needs required, thus showing the passion of worldly lusts whenever we can.

CHAPTER 6

Of the vision which a certain Elder saw
concerning the restless work of a brother

And that this is not done without the prompting of devils we are taught by the surest proofs, for when one very highly esteemed Elder was passing by the cell of a certain brother who was suffering from this mental disease of which we have spoken, as he was restlessly toiling in his daily occupations in building and repairing what was unnecessary, he watched him from a distance breaking a very hard stone with a heavy hammer, and saw a certain Ethiopian standing over him and together with him striking the blows of the hammer with joined and clasped hands, and urging him on with fiery incitements to diligence in the work. And so he stood still for a long while in astonishment at the force of the fierce demon and the deceitfulness of such an illusion. For when the brother was worn out and tired and wanted to rest and put an end to his toil, he was stimulated by the spirit's prompting and urged on to resume his hammer again and not to cease from devoting himself to the work which he had begun, so that being unweariedly supported by his incitements he did not feel the harm that so great labor was doing him. At last then the old man, disgusted at such a horrid mystification by a demon, turned aside to the brother's cell and saluted him, and asked, "What work is it, brother, that you are doing?" And he replied, "We are working at this awfully hard stone, and we can hardly break it at all." Whereupon the Elder replied: "You were right in saying 'we can,' for you were not alone, when you were striking it, but there was another with you whom you did not see, who was standing over you not so much to help you as urge you on with all his force."

And thus the fact that the disease of worldly vanity has not got hold of our hearts will be proved by no mere abstinence from those affairs which even if we want to engage in, we cannot carry out, nor by the despising of those matters which if we pursued them would make us remarkable in the front rank among spiritual persons as well as among worldly men, but only when we reject with inflexible firmness of mind whatever ministers to our power and seems to be veiled in a show of right. And in reality these things which seem trivial and of no consequence, and which we see to be permitted indifferently by those who belong to our calling, none the less by their character affect the soul than those more important things, which according to their condition usually intoxicate the senses of worldly people and which do not allow a monk to lay aside earthly impurities and aspire to God, on whom his attention should ever be fixed. For in his case even a slight separation from that highest good must be regarded as present death and most dangerous destruction.

And when the soul has been established in such a peaceful condition, and has been freed from the meshes of all carnal desires, and the purpose of the heart has been steadily fixed on that which is the only highest good, he will then fulfill this Apostolic precept: "Pray without ceasing" (1 Thes-

salonians 5:17), and, "In every place lifting up holy hands without wrath
and disputing" (1 Timothy 2:8). For when by this purity (if we can say
so) the thoughts of the soul are engrossed, and are re-fashioned out of
their earthly condition to bear a spiritual and angelic likeness, whatever
it receives, whatever it takes in hand, whatever it does, the prayer will
be perfectly pure and sincere.

CHAPTER 7

*A question how it is that it is harder work
to preserve than to originate good thoughts*

GERMANUS: If only we could keep as a lasting possession those spiritual
thoughts in the same way and with the same ease with which we generally
conceive their germs! For when they have been conceived in our hearts,
either through the recollection of the Scriptures or by the memory of
some spiritual actions, or by gazing upon heavenly mysteries, they vanish
all too soon and disappear by a sort of unnoticed flight. And when our
soul has discovered some other occasions for spiritual emotions, different ones again crowd in upon us, and those which we had grasped are
scattered, and lightly fly away so that the mind retaining no persistency,
and keeping of its own power no firm hand over holy thoughts, must
be thought, even when it does seem to retain them for a while, to have
conceived them at random and not of set purpose. For how can we think
that their rise should be ascribed to our own will, if they do not last
and remain with us? But that we may not owing to the consideration of
this question wander any further from the plan of the discourse we had
commenced, or delay any longer the explanation promised of the nature
of prayer, we will keep this for its own time, and ask to be informed at
once of the character of prayer, especially as the blessed Apostle exhorts
us at no time to cease from it, saying "Pray without ceasing." And so we
want to be taught first of its character, i.e., how prayer ought always to be
offered up, and then how we can secure this, whatever it is, and practice

it without ceasing. For that it cannot be done by any light purpose of heart, both daily experience and the explanation of your holiness show us, as you have laid it down that the aim of a monk, and the height of all perfection consist in the consummation of prayer.

CHAPTER 8
Of the different characters of prayer

ISAAC: I imagine that all kinds of prayers cannot be grasped without great purity of heart and soul and the illumination of the Holy Spirit. For there are as many of them as there can be conditions and characters produced in one soul or rather in all souls. And so although we know that owing to our dullness of heart we cannot see all kinds of prayers, yet we will try to relate them in some order, as far as our slender experience enables us to succeed. For according to the degree of the purity to which each soul attains, and the character of the state in which it is sunk owing to what happens to it, or is by its own efforts renewing itself, its very prayers will each moment be altered. And therefore it is quite clear that no one can always offer up uniform prayers. For everyone prays in one way when he is brisk, in another when he is oppressed with a weight of sadness or despair, in another when he is invigorated by spiritual achievements, in another when cast down by the burden of attacks, in another when he is asking pardon for his sins, in another when he asks to obtain grace or some virtue or else prays for the destruction of some sin, in another when he is pricked to the heart by the thought of hell and the fear of future judgment, in another when he is aglow with the hope and desire of good things to come, in another when he is taken up with affairs and dangers, in another when he is in peace and security, in another when he is enlightened by the revelation of heavenly mysteries, and in another when he is depressed by a sense of barrenness in virtues and dryness in feeling.

CHAPTER 9
Of the fourfold nature of prayer

And therefore, when we have laid this down with regard to the character of prayer—although not so fully as the importance of the subject
requires, but as fully as the exigencies of time permit, and at any rate
as our slender abilities admit, and our dullness of heart enables us—a
still greater difficulty now awaits us, viz., to expound one by one the different kinds of prayer, which the Apostle divides in a fourfold manner,
when he says as follows: "I exhort therefore first of all that supplications,
prayers, intercessions, thanksgivings be made" (1 Timothy 2:1). And we
cannot possibly doubt that this division was not idly made by the Apostle.
And to begin with, we must investigate what is meant by supplication,
by prayer, by intercession, and by thanksgiving. Next we must inquire
whether these four kinds are to be taken in hand by him who prays all at
once—i.e., are they all to be joined together in every prayer—or whether
they are to be offered up in turns and one by one, as, for instance, ought
at one time supplications, at another prayers, at another intercessions,
and at another thanksgivings to be offered, or should one man present
to God supplications, another prayers, another intercessions, another
thanksgivings, in accordance with that measure of age, to which each
soul is advancing by earnestness of purpose?

CHAPTER 10
Of the order of the different kinds
laid down with regard to the character of prayer

And so, to begin with, we must consider the actual force of the names and
words, and discuss what is the difference between prayer and supplication and intercession; then, in like manner, we must investigate whether
they are to be offered separately or all together; and in the third place
must examine whether the particular order which is thus arranged by the

Apostle's authority has anything further to teach the hearer, or whether the distinction simply is to be taken, and it should be considered that they were arranged by him indifferently in such a way—a thing which seems to me utterly absurd. For one must not believe that the Holy Spirit uttered anything casually or without reason through the Apostle. And so we will, as the Lord grants us, consider them in the same order in which we began.

CHAPTER 11
Of supplications

"I exhort therefore first of all that supplications be made." Supplication is an imploring or petition concerning sins, in which one who is sorry for his present or past deeds asks for pardon.

CHAPTER 12
Of prayer

Prayers are those by which we offer or vow something to God, what the Greeks call *euche*, i.e., a vow. For where we read in Greek, "*tas euchas mou to Kurio apodoso*," in Latin we read, "I will pay my vows unto the Lord" (Psalm 116:14), where according to the exact force of the words it may be thus represented: "I will pay my prayers unto the Lord." And this which we find in Ecclesiastes, "If you vow a vow unto the Lord, do not delay to pay it," is written in Greek likewise, "*ean euche euchen to Kurio*," i.e., "If you pray a prayer unto the Lord, do not delay to pay it" (Ecclesiastes 5:3), which will be fulfilled in this way by each one of us. We pray when we renounce this world and promise that, being dead to all worldly actions and the life of this world, we will serve the Lord with full purpose of heart. We pray when we promise that, despising secular honors and scorning earthly riches, we will cleave to the Lord in all sorrow of heart and humility of spirit. We pray when we promise that we will ever maintain the most perfect purity of body and steadfast patience, or when we vow that we will utterly root out of our heart the roots of anger or of sorrow that works death. And if, enervated by sloth and returning to our former sins, we fail to do this, we shall be guilty as regards our prayers and vows, and these words will apply to us: "It is better not to vow, than to vow and not to pay," which can be rendered in accordance with the Greek: "It is better for you not to pray than to pray and not to pay" (Ecclesiastes 5:4).

CHAPTER 13

Of intercession

In the third place stand intercessions, which we are wont to offer up for others also, while we are filled with fervor of spirit, making request either for those dear to us or for the peace of the whole world, and to use the Apostle's own phrase, we pray "for all men, for kings and all that are in authority" (1 Timothy 2:1–2).

CHAPTER 14

Of thanksgiving

Then in the fourth place there stand thanksgivings, which the mind in ineffable transports offers up to God, either when it recalls God's past benefits, or when it contemplates his present ones, or when it looks forward to those great ones in the future which God has prepared for them that love him. And with this purpose, too, sometimes we are wont to pour forth richer prayers, while, as we gaze with pure eyes on those rewards of the saints which are laid up in store hereafter, our spirit is stimulated to offer up unspeakable thanks to God with boundless joy.

CHAPTER 15

Whether these four kinds of prayers are necessary
for everyone to offer all at once or separately and in turns

And of these four kinds, although sometimes occasions arise for richer
and fuller prayers (for from the class of supplications which arises from
sorrow for sin, and from the kind of prayer which flows from confidence
in our offerings and the performance of our vows in accordance with a
pure conscience, and from the intercession which proceeds from fervor
of love, and from the thanksgiving which is born of the consideration of
God's blessings and his greatness and goodness, we know that oftentimes
there proceed most fervent and ardent prayers so that it is clear that all
these kinds of prayer of which we have spoken are found to be useful and
needful for all men, so that in one and the same man his changing feelings
will give utterance to pure and fervent petitions now of supplications,
now of prayers, now of intercessions) yet the first seems to belong more
especially to beginners, who are still troubled by the stings and recollection of their sins; the second to those who have already attained some
loftiness of mind in their spiritual progress and the quest of virtue; the
third to those who fulfil the completion of their vows by their works, and
are so stimulated to intercede for others also through the consideration
of their weakness, and the earnestness of their love; the fourth to those
who have already torn from their hearts the guilty thorns of conscience,
and thus being now free from care can contemplate with a pure mind the
beneficence of God and his compassions, which he has either granted
in the past, or is giving in the present, or preparing for the future, and
thus are borne onward with fervent hearts to that ardent prayer which
cannot be embraced or expressed by the mouth of men.

Sometimes, however, the mind which is advancing to that perfect
state of purity, and which is already beginning to be established in it, will
take in all these at one and the same time, and like some incomprehensible and all-devouring flame, dart through them all and offer up to God
inexpressible prayers of the purest force, which the Spirit itself, interven-

ing with groanings that cannot be uttered, while we ourselves understand not, pours forth to God, grasping at that hour and ineffably pouring forth in its supplications things so great that they cannot be uttered with the mouth nor even at any other time be recollected by the mind.

And thence it comes that in whatever degree anyone stands, he is found sometimes to offer up pure and devout prayers; as even in that first and lowly station which has to do with the recollection of future judgment, he who still remains under the punishment of terror and the fear of judgment is so smitten with sorrow for the time being that he is filled with no less keenness of spirit from the richness of his supplications than he who through the purity of his heart gazes on and considers the blessings of God and is overcome with ineffable joy and delight. For, as the Lord himself says, he begins to love the more, who knows that he has been forgiven the more (Luke 7:47).

CHAPTER 16

Of the kinds of prayer to which we ought to direct ourselves

Yet we ought by advancing in life and attaining to virtue to aim rather at those kinds of prayer which are poured forth either from the contemplation of the good things to come or from fervor of love, or which at least, to speak more humbly and in accordance with the measure of beginners, arise for the acquirement of some virtue or the extinction of some fault. For otherwise we shall not possibly attain to those sublimer kinds of supplication of which we spoke, unless our mind has been little by little and by degrees raised through the regular course of those intercessions.

CHAPTER 17

How the four kinds of supplication were originated by the Lord

These four kinds of supplication the Lord himself, by his own example, vouchsafed to originate for us, so that in this too he might fulfil that which was said of him, "which Jesus began both to do and to teach" (Acts 1:1). For he made use of the class of supplication when he said, "Father, if it be possible, let this cup pass from me" (Matthew 26:39); or this which is chanted in his Person in the Psalm, "My God, My God, look upon me, why have you forsaken me" (Psalm 22:2); and others like it. It is prayer where he says, "I have magnified you upon the earth; I have finished the work which you gave me to do" (John 17:4), and this: "And for their sakes, I sanctify myself, that they also may be sanctified in the truth" (John 17:19). It is intercession when he says, "Father, those whom you have given me, I will that they also may be with me, that they may see my glory which you have given me" (John 17:24); or at any rate when he says, "Father, forgive them, for they know not what they do" (Luke 23:34). It is thanksgiving when he says, "I confess to you, Father, Lord of heaven and earth, that you have hid these things from the wise and prudent, and have revealed them unto babes. Even so, Father, for so it seemed good in your sight" (Matthew 11:25–26), or at least when he says: "Father, I thank you that you have heard me. But I knew that you hear me always" (John 11:41–42).

But though our Lord made a distinction between these four kinds of prayers as to be offered separately and one by one according to the scheme which we know of, yet that they can all be embraced in a perfect prayer at one and the same time he showed by his own example in that prayer which at the close of St. John's gospel we read that he offered up with such fullness. From the words of which (as it is too long to repeat it all) the careful inquirer can discover by the order of the passage that this is so. And the Apostle also in his Epistle to the Philippians has expressed the same meaning, by putting these four kinds of prayers in a slightly different order, and has shown that they ought sometimes to be offered together in the fervor of a single prayer, saying as follows: "But in everything by prayer and supplication with thanksgiving let your requests be made known unto God" (Philippians 4:6). And by this he wanted us especially to understand that in prayer and supplication thanksgiving ought to be mingled with our requests.

CHAPTER 18
Of the Lord's Prayer

And so there follows after these different kinds of supplication a still more sublime and exalted condition which is brought about by the contemplation of God alone and by fervent love, by which the mind, transporting and flinging itself into love for him, addresses God most familiarly as its own Father with a piety of its own. And that we ought earnestly to seek after this condition the formula of the Lord's prayer teaches us, saying, "Our Father." When then we confess with our own mouths that the God and Lord of the universe is our Father, we profess forthwith that we have been called from our condition as slaves to the adoption of sons, adding next, "which art in heaven," that, by shunning with the utmost horror all lingering in this present life, which we pass upon this earth as a pilgrimage, and what separates us by a great distance from our Father, we may the rather hasten with all eagerness to that country where we confess that our Father dwells, and may not allow anything of this kind, which would make us unworthy of this our profession and the dignity of an adoption of this kind, and so deprive us as a disgrace to our Father's inheritance, and make us incur the wrath of his justice and severity. To which state and condition of sonship when we have advanced, we shall forthwith be inflamed with the piety which belongs to good sons, so that we shall bend all our energies to the advance not of our own profit, but of our Father's glory, saying to him, "Hallowed be thy name," testifying that our desire and our joy is his glory, becoming imitators of him who said: "He who speaks of himself seeks his own glory. But he who seeks the glory of him who sent him, the same is true, and there is no unrighteousness in him" (John 7:18). Finally the chosen vessel being filled with this feeling wished that he could be anathema from Christ (Romans 9:3), if only the people belonging to him might be increased and multiplied, and the salvation of the whole nation of Israel accrue to the glory of his Father; for with all assurance could he wish to die for Christ as he knew that no one perished for life. And again he says, "We rejoice when we are weak but ye are strong" (2 Corinthians 13:9). And what wonder if the chosen vessel wished to be anathema from Christ for the sake of Christ's glory and the conversion of his own brethren and the privilege of the nation, when the prophet Micah wished that he might be a liar and a stranger to the inspiration of the Holy Spirit, if only the people of the Jews might escape those plagues and the going forth into captivity which he had announced in his prophecy, saying, "Would that I were not a man that has the Spirit, and that I rather spoke a lie" (Micah 2:11)—to pass over that wish of the Lawgiver, who did not refuse to die together with his brethren who were doomed to death, saying: "I beseech you, O Lord; this people has sinned a heinous sin; either forgive them this trespass, or if you do not, blot me out of your book which you have written" (Exodus 32:31–32). But where it is said, "Hallowed be thy name," it may also be very fairly taken in this way: "The hallowing of God is our perfection." And so when we say to him, "Hallowed be thy name," we say, in other words, make us, O Father, such that we maybe able both to understand and take in what the hallowing of you is, or at any rate that you may be seen to be hallowed in our spiritual converse. And this is effectually fulfilled in our case when "men see our good works, and glorify our Father which is in heaven" (Matthew 5:16).

CHAPTER 19
Of the clause "Thy kingdom come"

The second petition of the pure heart desires that the kingdom of its Father may come at once; viz., either that whereby Christ reigns day by day in the saints (which comes to pass when the devil's rule is cast out of our hearts by the destruction of foul sins, and God begins to hold sway over us by the sweet odor of virtues, and, fornication being overcome, charity reigns in our hearts together with tranquillity, when rage is conquered; and humility, when pride is trampled under foot), or else that which is promised in due time to all who are perfect, and to all the sons of God, when it will be said to them by Christ: "Come you blessed of my Father, inherit the kingdom prepared for you from the foundation of the world" (Matthew 25:34), as the heart with fixed and steadfast gaze, so to speak, yearns and longs for it and says to him, "Thy kingdom come." For it knows by the witness of its own conscience that when he shall appear, it will presently share his lot. For no guilty person would dare either to say or to wish for this, for no one would want to face the tribunal of the Judge, who knew that at his coming he would forthwith receive not the prize or reward of his merits but only punishment.

CHAPTER 20
Of the clause "Thy will be done"

The third petition is that of sons: "Thy will be done, as in heaven, so on earth." There can now be no grander prayer than to wish that earthly things may be made equal with things heavenly: for what else is it to say, "Thy will be done, as in heaven, so on earth," than to ask that men may be like angels, and that as God's will is ever fulfilled by them in heaven, so also all those who are on earth may do not their own but his will? This, too, no one could say from the heart, but only one who believed that God disposes for our good all things which are seen, whether fortunate or unfortunate, and that he is more careful and provident for our good and salvation than we ourselves are for ourselves. Or at any rate it may be taken in this way: The will of God is the salvation of all men, according to these words of the blessed Paul, "Who wills all men to be saved and to come to the knowledge of the truth" (1 Timothy 2:4). Of which will also the prophet Isaiah says in the Person of God the Father: "And all your will shall be done" (Isaiah 46:10). When we say, then, "Thy will be done as in heaven so on earth," we pray in other words for this, viz., that as those who are in heaven, so also may all those who dwell on earth be saved, O Father, by the knowledge of you.

CHAPTER 21
Of our supersubstantial or daily bread

Next, "Give us this day our bread which is *epiousion*," i.e., "supersubstantial," which another Evangelist calls "daily."* The former indicates the quality of its nobility and substance, in virtue of which it is above all substances and the loftiness of its grandeur and holiness exceeds all creatures, while the latter intimates the purpose of its use and value. For where it says "daily," it shows that without it we cannot live a spiritual life for a single day. Where it says "today," it shows that it must be received daily, and that yesterday's supply of it is not enough, but that it must be given to us today also in like manner. And our daily need of it suggests to us that we ought at all times to offer up this prayer, because there is no day on which we have no need to strengthen the heart of our inner man, by eating and receiving it, although the expression used, "today," may be taken to apply to his present life, i.e., while we are living in this

---

* Here Cassian is relying entirely on Jerome's revised text of the Latin, which has *supersubstantialis* in Matthew 6:11, as the rendering of *epiousios* but translates the same word by *quotidianum* in the parallel passage in Luke 11:3. It is curious that Cassian should have been thus misled, with his knowledge of Greek, as well as his acquaintance with the old Latin version which has *quotidianum* in both gospels.

world supply us with this bread. "For we know that it will be given to those who deserve it by you hereafter, but we ask that you would grant it to us today, because unless it has been vouchsafed to a man to receive it in this life, he will never be partaker of it in that."

CHAPTER 22

Of the clause "Forgive us our debts, etc."

"And forgive us our debts, as we also forgive our debtors." O unspeakable mercy of God, which has not only given us a form of prayer and taught us a system of life acceptable to him, and by the requirements of the form given, in which he charged us always to pray, has torn up the roots of both anger and sorrow, but also gives to those who pray an opportunity and reveals to them a way by which they may move a merciful and kindly judgment of God to be pronounced over them, and which somehow gives us a power by which we can moderate the sentence of our Judge, drawing him to forgive our offenses by the example of our forgiveness, when we say to him, "Forgive us as we also forgive."

And so without anxiety and in confidence from this prayer, a man may ask for pardon of his own offenses if he has been forgiving towards his own debtors, and not towards those of his Lord. For some of us, which is very bad, are inclined to show ourselves calm and most merciful in regard to those things which are done to God's detriment, however great the crimes may be, but to be found most hard and inexorable exactors of debts to ourselves even in the case of the most trifling wrongs. Whoever then does not from his heart forgive his brother who has offended him, by this prayer calls down upon himself not forgiveness but condemnation, and by his own profession asks that he himself may be judged more severely, saying, "Forgive me as I also have forgiven." And if he is repaid according to his own request, what else will follow but that he will be punished after his own example with implacable wrath and a sentence that cannot be remitted? And so if we want to be judged mercifully, we ought also to be merciful towards those who have sinned against us. For only so much will be remitted to us, as we have remitted to those who have injured us however spitefully. And some, dreading this, when this prayer is chanted by all the people in church, silently omit this clause, for fear lest they may seem by their own utterance to bind themselves rather than to excuse themselves, as they do not understand that it is in vain that they try to offer these quibbles to the Judge of all men, who has willed to show us beforehand how he will judge his suppliants. For as he does not wish to be found harsh and inexorable towards them, he has marked out the manner of his judgment, that just as we desire to be judged by him, so we should also judge our brethren, if they have wronged us in anything, for, "He shall have judgment without mercy who has shown no mercy" (James 2:13).

CHAPTER 23
Of the clause "Lead us not into temptation"

Next there follows, "And lead us not into temptation," on which there arises no unimportant question, for if we pray that we may not be suffered to be tempted, how then will our power of endurance be proved, according to this text: "Everyone who is not tempted is not proved" (Sirach 34:10). And again: "Blessed is the man that endures temptation" (James 1:12). The clause, then, "Lead us not into temptation," does not mean this—viz., do not permit us ever to be tempted—but do not permit us, when we fall into temptation, to be overcome. For Job was tempted, but was not led into temptation. For he did not ascribe folly to God nor blasphemy, nor with impious mouth did he yield to that wish of the tempter toward which he was drawn. Abraham was tempted, Joseph was tempted, but neither of them was led into temptation, for neither of them yielded his consent to the tempter. Next there follows: "But deliver us from evil," i.e., do not suffer us to be tempted by the devil above that we are able, but "make with the temptation a way also of escape that we may be able to bear it" (1 Corinthians 10:13).

CHAPTER 24

How we ought not to ask for other things, except only those which are contained in the limits of the Lord's Prayer

You see, then, what is the method and form of prayer proposed to us by the Judge himself, who is to be prayed to by it, a form in which there is contained no petition for riches, no thought of honors, no request for power and might, no mention of bodily health and of temporal life. For he who is the Author of Eternity would have men ask of him nothing uncertain, nothing paltry, and nothing temporal. And so a man will offer the greatest insult to his Majesty and Bounty, if he leaves on one side these eternal petitions and chooses rather to ask of him something transitory and uncertain; and will also incur the indignation rather than the propitiation of the Judge by the pettiness of his prayer.

CHAPTER 25

Of the character of the sublimer prayer

This prayer, then, though it seems to contain all the fullness of perfection, as being what was originated and appointed by the Lord's own authority, yet lifts those to whom it belongs to that still higher condition of which we spoke above, and carries them on by a loftier stage to that ardent prayer which is known and tried by but very few, and which to speak more truly is ineffable; which transcends all human thoughts, and is distinguished, I will not say by any sound of the voice, but by no movement of the tongue, or utterance of words, but which the mind enlightened by the infusion of that heavenly light describes in no human and confined language, but pours forth richly as from copious fountain in an accumulation of thoughts, and ineffably utters to God, expressing in the shortest possible space of time such great things that the mind, when it returns to its usual condition, cannot easily utter or relate. And this condition our Lord also similarly prefigured by the form of those supplications which, when he retired alone in the mountain he is said to have poured forth in silence, and when being in an agony of prayer he shed forth even drops of blood, as an example of a purpose which it is hard to imitate.

CHAPTER 26
Of the different causes of conviction

But who is able, with whatever experience he may be endowed, to give a sufficient account of the varieties and reasons and grounds of conviction, by which the mind is inflamed and set on fire and incited to pure and most fervent prayers? And of these we will now by way of specimen set forth a few, as far as we can by God's enlightenment recollect them. For sometimes a verse of any one of the Psalms gives us an occasion of ardent prayer while we are singing. Sometimes the harmonious modulation of a brother's voice stirs up the minds of dullards to intense supplication. We know also that the enunciation and the reverence of the chanter adds greatly to the fervor of those who stand by. Moreover the exhortation of a perfect man and a spiritual conference has often raised the affections of those present to the richest prayer. We know, too, that by the death of a brother or some one dear to us, we are no less carried away to full conviction. The recollection also of our coldness and carelessness has sometimes aroused in us a healthful fervor of spirit. And in this way no one can doubt that numberless opportunities are not wanting, by which through God's grace the coldness and sleepiness of our minds can be shaken off.

CHAPTER 27
Of the different sorts of conviction

But how and in what way those very convictions are produced from the inmost recesses of the soul, it is no less difficult to trace out. For often through some inexpressible delight and keenness of spirit the fruit of a most salutary conviction arises, so that it actually breaks forth into shouts owing to the greatness of its incontrollable joy; and the delight of the heart and greatness of exultation makes itself heard even in the cell of a neighbor. But sometimes the mind hides itself in complete silence within the secrets of a profound quiet, so that the amazement of a sudden illumination chokes all sounds of words and the overawed spirit either keeps all its feelings to itself or loses them and pours forth its desires to God with groanings that cannot be uttered. But sometimes it is filled with such overwhelming conviction and grief that it cannot express it except by floods of tears.

CHAPTER 28

A question about the fact
that a plentiful supply of tears is not in our own power

GERMANUS: My own poor self, indeed, is not altogether ignorant of this feeling of conviction. For often when tears arise at the recollection of my faults, I have been by the Lord's visitation so refreshed by this ineffable joy which you describe that the greatness of the joy has assured me that I ought not to despair of their forgiveness. Than which state of mind I think there is nothing more sublime, if only it could be recalled at our own will. For sometimes when I am desirous to stir myself up with all my power to the same conviction and tears, and place before my eyes all my faults and sins, I am unable to bring back that copiousness of tears, and so my eyes are dry and hard like some hardest flint, so that not a single tear trickles from them. And so in proportion as I congratulate myself on that copiousness of tears, just so do I mourn that I cannot bring it back again whenever I wish.

CHAPTER 29

The answer on the varieties of conviction which spring from tears

ISAAC: Not every kind of shedding of tears is produced by one feeling or one virtue. For in one way does that weeping originate which is caused by the pricks of our sins smiting our heart, of which we read, "I have labored in my groanings, every night I will wash my bed; I will water my couch with my tears" (Psalm 6:7). And again: "Let tears run down like a torrent day and night: give yourself no rest, and let not the apple of your eye cease" (Lamentations 2:18). In another, that which arises from the contemplation of eternal good things and the desire of that future glory, owing to which even richer well-springs of tears burst forth from uncontrollable delights and boundless exultation, while our soul is athirst for the mighty Living God, saying, "When shall I come and appear before the presence of God? My tears have been my meat day and night" (Psalm 43:3–4), declaring with daily crying and lamentation: "Woe is me that my sojourning is prolonged," and, "Too long has my soul been a sojourner" (Psalm 120:5–6). In another way do the tears flow forth, which without any conscience of deadly sin, yet still proceed from the fear of hell and the recollection of that terrible judgment, with the terror of which the prophet was smitten and prayed to God, saying: "Enter not into judgment with your servant, for in your sight shall no man living be justified" (Psalm 143:2).

There is, too, another kind of tears, which are caused not by knowledge of one's self but by the hardness and sins of others; whereby Samuel is described as having wept for Saul, and both the Lord in the gospel and Jeremiah in former days for the city of Jerusalem, the latter thus saying: "Oh, that my head were water and my eyes a fountain of tears! And I will weep day and night for the slain of the daughter of my people" (Jeremiah 9:1). Or also such as were those tears of which we hear in the hundred and first Psalm: "For I have eaten ashes for my bread, and mingled my cup with weeping" (Psalm 102:10). And these were certainty not caused by the same feeling as those which arise in the sixth Psalm from the person of the penitent, but were due to the anxieties of this life and its distresses and losses, by which the righteous who are living in this world are oppressed. And this is clearly shown not only by the words of the Psalm itself, but also by its title, which runs as follows in the character of that poor person of whom it is said in the gospel that, "Blessed are the poor in spirit, for theirs is the kingdom of heaven" (Matthew 5:3), "A prayer of the poor when he was in distress and poured forth his prayer to God" (Psalm 102:1).

CHAPTER 30

How tears ought not to be squeezed out
when they do not flow spontaneously

From these tears those are vastly different which are squeezed out from dry eyes while the heart is hard. And although we cannot believe that these are altogether fruitless (for the attempt to shed them is made with a good intention, especially by those who have not yet been able to attain to perfect knowledge or to be thoroughly cleansed from the stains of past or present sins), yet certainly the flow of tears ought not to be thus forced out by those who have already advanced to the love of virtue, nor should the weeping of the outward man be with great labor attempted, as even if it is produced it will never attain the rich copiousness of spontaneous tears. For it will rather cast down the soul of the suppliant by his endeavors, and humiliate him, and plunge him in human affairs, and draw him away from the celestial heights, wherein the awed mind of one who prays should be steadfastly fixed, and will force it to relax its hold on its prayers and grow sick from barren and forced tears.

CHAPTER 31

The opinion of Abbot Antony on the condition of prayer

And that you may see the character of true prayer I will give you not
my own opinion but that of the blessed Antony: whom we have known
sometimes to have been so persistent in prayer that often as he was praying in a transport of mind, when the sunrise began to appear, we have
heard him in the fervor of his spirit declaiming, "Why do you hinder
me, O sun, who are arising for this very purpose, viz., to withdraw me
from the brightness of this true light?" And his also is this heavenly and
more than human utterance on the end of prayer: "That is not," said he,
"a perfect prayer, wherein a monk understands himself and the words
which he prays." And if we too, as far as our slender ability allows, may
venture to add anything to this splendid utterance, we will bring forward
the marks of prayer which are heard from the Lord, as far as we have
tried them.

CHAPTER 32

Of the proof of prayer being heard

When, while we are praying, no hesitation intervenes and breaks down
the confidence of our petition by a sort of despair, but we feel that by
pouring forth our prayer we have obtained what we are asking for, we
have no doubt that our prayers have effectually reached God. For so far
will one be heard and obtain an answer, as he believes that he is regarded
by God, and that God can grant it. For this saying of our Lord cannot
be retracted: "Whatsoever you ask when ye pray, believe that you shall
receive, and they shall come to you" (Mark 11:24).

CHAPTER 33

An objection that the confidence of being thus heard
as described belongs only to saints

GERMANUS: We certainly believe that this confidence of being heard
flows from purity of conscience, but for us, whose heart is still smitten
by the pricks of sins, how can we have it, as we have no merits to plead
for us, whereby we might confidently presume that our prayers would
be heard?

CHAPTER 34

Answer on the different reasons for prayer being heard

ISAAC: That there are different reasons for prayer being heard, in accordance with the varied and changing condition of souls, the words of
the gospels and of the prophets teach us. For you have the fruits of an
answer pointed out by our Lord's words in the case of the agreement of
two persons; as it is said: "If two of you shall agree upon earth touching
anything for which they shall ask, it shall be done for them of my Father
which is in heaven" (Matthew 18:19). You have another in the fullness
of faith, which is compared to a grain of mustard-seed. "For," he says, "if
you have faith as a grain of mustard seed, ye shall say unto this mountain:
Be removed, and it shall be removed; and nothing shall be impossible to
you" (Matthew 17:19). You have it in continuance in prayer, which the
Lord's words call, by reason of unwearied perseverance in petitioning,
importunity: "For, verily, I say unto you that if not because of his friendship, yet because of his importunity he will rise and give him as much
as he needs" (Luke 11:8). You have it in the fruits of almsgiving: "Shut
up alms in the heart of the poor, and it shall pray for you in the time
of tribulation" (Sirach 29:12). You have it in the purifying of life and in
works of mercy, as it is said: "Loose the bands of wickedness, undo the
bundles that oppress" (Isaiah 58:6); and after a few words in which the

barrenness of an unfruitful fast is rebuked, "Then," he says, "you shall call and the Lord shall hear you; you shall cry, and he shall say, Here am I" (Isaiah 58:9). Sometimes also excess of trouble causes it to be heard, as it is said: "When I was in trouble I called unto the Lord, and he heard me" (Psalm 120:1). And again: "Afflict not the stranger, for if he cries unto me, I will hear him, for I am merciful" (Exodus 22:21, 27).

You see, then, in how many ways the gift of an answer may be obtained, so that no one need be crushed by the despair of his conscience for securing those things which are salutary and eternal. For if in contemplating our wretchedness I admit that we are utterly destitute of all those virtues which we mentioned above, and that we have neither that laudable agreement of two persons, nor that faith which is compared to a grain of mustard seed, nor those works of piety which the prophet describes, surely we cannot be without that importunity which he supplies to all who desire it, owing to which alone the Lord promises that he will give whatever he has been prayed to give. And therefore we ought without unbelieving hesitation to persevere, and not to have the least doubt that by continuing in them we shall obtain all those things which we have asked according to the mind of God. For the Lord, in his desire to grant what is heavenly and eternal, urges us to constrain him as it were by our importunity, as he not only does not despise or reject the importunate, but actually welcomes and praises them, and most graciously promises to grant whatever they have perseveringly hoped for; saying, "Ask and you shall receive: seek and you shall find: knock and it shall be opened unto you. For every one that asks receives, and he that seeks finds, and to him that knocks it shall be opened" (Luke 9:9–10). And again: "All things whatsoever you shall ask in prayer believing you shall receive, and nothing shall be impossible to you" (Matthew 21:22; 17:20).

And therefore even if all the grounds for being heard which we have mentioned are altogether wanting, at any rate the earnestness of importunity may animate us, as this is placed in the power of any one who wills without the difficulties of any merits or labors. But let not any suppliant doubt that he certainly will not be heard, so long as he doubts whether he is heard. But that this also shall be sought from the Lord unweariedly, we are taught by the example of the blessed Daniel, as, though he was heard from the first day on which he began to pray, he only obtained the result of his petition after twenty-one days (Daniel 10:2). Wherefore we also ought not to grow slack in the earnestness of the prayers we have begun if we fancy that the answer comes but slowly, for fear lest perhaps the gift of the answer be in God's providence delayed, or the angel, who was to bring the Divine blessing to us, may when he comes forth from the Presence of the Almighty be hindered by the resistance of the devil, as it is certain that he cannot transmit and bring to us the desired boon, if he finds that we slack off from the earnestness of the petition made. And this would certainly have happened to the above mentioned prophet, unless he had with incomparable steadfastness prolonged and persevered in his prayers until the twenty-first day.

Let us, then, not be at all cast down by despair from the confidence of this faith of ours, even when we fancy that we are far from having obtained what we prayed for, and let us not have any doubts about the Lord's promise where he says, "All things, whatsoever you shall ask in prayer believing, you shall receive" (Matthew 21:22). For it is well for us to consider this saying of the blessed Evangelist John, by which the ambiguity of this question is clearly solved: "This is," he says, "the confidence which we have in him, that whatsoever we ask according to his will, he hears us" (1 John 5:16). He bids us, then, have a full and undoubting confidence of the answer only in those things which are not for our own advantage or for temporal comforts, but are in conformity to the Lord's will. And we are also taught to put this into our prayers by the Lord's Prayer, where we say "Thy will be done"—thine, not ours. For if we also remember these words of the Apostle that "We know not what to pray for as we ought" (Romans 8:26), we shall see that we sometimes ask for things opposed to our salvation and that we are most providentially refused our requests by him who sees what is good for us with greater right and truth than we can. And it is clear that this also happened to the teacher of the Gentiles when he prayed that the messenger of Satan who had been for his good allowed by the Lord's will to buffet him, might be removed, saying: "For which I besought the Lord thrice that he might depart from me. And he said unto me, My grace is sufficient for you, for strength is made perfect in weakness" (2 Corinthians 12:8–9).

And this feeling even our Lord expressed when he prayed in the character of man which he had taken, that he might give us a form of prayer as other things also by his example; saying thus: "Father, if it be possible, let this cup pass from me: nevertheless not as I will but as you will" (Matthew 26:39), though certainly his will was not discordant with his Father's will, "For he had come to save what was lost and to give his life a ransom for many" (Matthew 18:11; 20:28), as he himself says: "No man takes my life from me, but I lay it down of myself. I have power to lay it down, and I have power to take it again" (John 10:18). In which character there is in the [fortieth] Psalm the following sung by the blessed David, of the unity of will which he ever maintained with the Father: "To do your will: O my God, I am willing" (Psalm 40:9).

For even if we read of the Father: "For God so loved the world that he gave his only begotten Son" (1 John 3:16), we find none the less of the Son, "Who gave himself for our sins" (Galatians 1:4). And as it is said of the One, "Who spared not his own Son, but gave him for all of us" (Romans 8:32), so it is written of the other, "He was offered because he himself willed it" (Isaiah 53:7). And it is shown that the will of the Father and of the Son is in all things one, so that even in the actual mystery of the Lord's resurrection we are taught that there was no discord of operation. For just as the blessed Apostle declares that the Father brought about the resurrection of his body, saying, "And God the Father, who raised him from the dead" (Galatians 1:1), so also the Son testifies that he himself will raise again the Temple of his body, saying, "Destroy this temple, and in three days I will raise it up again" (John 2:19).

And therefore we, being instructed by all these examples of our Lord which have been enumerated, ought to end our supplications also with the same prayer, and always to subjoin this clause to all our petitions: "Nevertheless not as I will, but as you will" (Matthew 26:39). But it is clear enough that one who does not pray with attention of mind cannot observe that threefold reverence which is usually practiced in the assemblies of the brethren at the close of service.

CHAPTER 35
Of prayer to be offered within the chamber and with the door shut

Before all things, however, we ought most carefully to observe the Evangelic precept which tells us to enter into our chamber and shut the door and pray to our Father, which may be fulfilled by us as follows: We pray within our chamber when, removing our hearts inwardly from the din of all thoughts and anxieties, we disclose our prayers in secret and in closest intercourse to the Lord. We pray with closed doors when with closed lips and complete silence we pray to the searcher not of words but of hearts. We pray in secret when from the heart and fervent mind we disclose our petitions to God alone, so that no hostile powers are even able to discover the character of our petition. Wherefore we should pray in complete silence, not only to avoid distracting the brethren standing near by our whispers or louder utterances, and disturbing the thoughts of those who are praying, but also that the purport of our petition may be concealed from our enemies who are especially on the watch against us while we are praying. For so we shall fulfill this injunction: "Keep the doors of your mouth from her who sleeps in your bosom" (Micah 7:5).

CHAPTER 36
Of the value of short and silent prayer

Wherefore we ought to pray often but briefly, lest if we are long about it our crafty foe may succeed in implanting something in our heart. For that is the true sacrifice, as "the sacrifice of God is a broken spirit." This is the salutary offering, these are pure drink offerings, that is the "sacrifice of righteousness," the "sacrifice of praise," these are true and fat victims, "holocausts full of marrow," which are offered by contrite and humble hearts, and which those who practise this control and fervor of spirit, of which we have spoken, with effectual power can sing: "Let my prayer be set forth in your sight as the incense: let the lifting up of my hands be an evening sacrifice" (Psalm 51:19, 21; 50:23; 66:15; 141:2). But the approach of the right hour and of night warns us that we ought with fitting devotion to do this very thing, of which, as our slender ability allowed, we seem to have propounded a great deal, and to have prolonged our conference considerably, though we believe that we have discoursed very little when the magnificence and difficulty of the subject are taken into account.

With these words of the holy Isaac we were dazzled rather than satisfied, and after evening service had been held, rested our limbs for a short time, and intending at the first dawn again to return under promise of a fuller discussion departed, rejoicing over the acquisition of these precepts as well as over the assurance of his promises. Since we felt that though the excellence of prayer had been shown to us, still we had not yet understood from his discourse its nature, and the power by which continuance in it might be gained and kept.

The Second Conference of Abbot Isaac
On Prayer

CHAPTER 1
Introduction

Among the sublime customs of the anchorites which by God's help have
been set forth, although in plain and unadorned style, the course of our
narration compels us to insert and find a place for something which may
seem, so to speak, to cause a blemish on a fair body: although I have no
doubt that by it no small instruction on the image of Almighty God of
which we read in Genesis will be conferred on some of the simpler sort,
especially when the grounds are considered of a doctrine so important
that men cannot be ignorant of it without terrible blasphemy and serious
harm to the Catholic faith.

CHAPTER 2
Of the custom which is kept up in the Province of Egypt
for signifying the time of Easter

In the country of Egypt this custom is by ancient tradition observed that,
when Epiphany is past—which the priests of that province regard as the
time both of our Lord's baptism and also of his birth in the flesh, and

so celebrate the commemoration of either mystery not separately as in the Western provinces but on the single festival of this day—letters are sent from the Bishop of Alexandria through all the Churches of Egypt, by which the beginning of Lent, and the day of Easter are pointed out not only in all the cities but also in all the monasteries.

In accordance, then, with this custom, a very few days after the previous conference had been held with Abbot Isaac, there arrived the festal letters of Theophilus the Bishop of the aforesaid city, in which together with the announcement of Easter he considered as well the foolish heresy of the Anthropomorphites at great length, and abundantly refuted it. And this was received by almost all the body of monks residing in the whole province of Egypt with such bitterness, owing to their simplicity and error, that the greater part of the Elders decreed that on the contrary the aforesaid Bishop ought to be abhorred by the whole body of the brethren as tainted with heresy of the worst kind, because he seemed to impugn the teaching of holy Scripture by the denial that Almighty God was formed in the fashion of a human figure, though Scripture teaches with perfect clearness that Adam was created in his image. Lastly, this letter was rejected also by those who were living in the desert of Scete and who excelled all who were in the monasteries of Egypt, in perfection and in knowledge, so that except Abbot Paphnutius, the presbyter of our congregation, not one of the other presbyters who presided over the other three churches in the same desert would suffer it to be even read or repeated at all in their meetings.

CHAPTER 3

*Of Abbot Sarapion and the heresy of the Anthropomorphites
into which he fell in the error of simplicity*

Among those then who were caught by this mistaken notion was one named Sarapion, a man of long-standing strictness of life, and one who was altogether perfect in actual discipline, whose ignorance with regard to the view of the doctrine first mentioned was so far a stumbling block to all who held the true faith, as he himself outstripped almost all the monks both in the merits of his life and in the length of time (he had been there).

And when this man could not be brought back to the way of the right faith by many exhortations of the holy presbyter Paphnutius, because this view seemed to him a novelty, and one that was not ever known to or handed down by his predecessors, it chanced that a certain deacon, a man of very great learning named Photinus, arrived from the region of Cappadocia with the desire of visiting the brethren living in the same desert: whom the blessed Paphnutius received with the warmest welcome, and in order to confirm the faith which had been stated in the letters of the aforesaid Bishop, placed him in the midst and asked him before all the brethren how the Catholic Churches throughout the East interpreted the passage in Genesis where it says, "Let us make man after our image and likeness" (Genesis 1:26). And when he explained that the image and likeness of God was taken by all the leaders of the churches not according to the base sound of the letters, but spiritually, and supported this very fully and by many passages of Scripture, and showed that nothing of this sort could happen to that infinite and incomprehensible and invisible glory, so that it could be comprised in a human form and likeness, since its nature is incorporeal and uncompounded and simple, and what can neither be apprehended by the eyes nor conceived by the mind, at length the old man was shaken by the numerous and very weighty assertions of this most learned man, and was drawn to the faith of the Catholic tradition.

And when both Abbot Paphnutius and all of us were filled with intense delight at his adhesion, for this reason, viz., that the Lord had not permitted a man of such age and crowned with such virtues, and one who erred only from ignorance and rustic simplicity, to wander from the path of the right faith up to the very last. And when we arose to give thanks, and were all together offering up our prayers to the Lord, the old man was so bewildered in mind during his prayer because he felt that the Anthropomorphic image of the Godhead which he used to set before himself in prayer, was banished from his heart, that on a sudden he burst into a flood of bitter tears and continual sobs, and cast himself down on the ground and exclaimed with strong groanings: "Alas! Wretched man that I am! They have taken away my God from me, and I have now none to lay hold of; and whom to worship and address I know not." By which scene we were terribly disturbed, and moreover with the effect of the former Conference still remaining in our hearts, we returned to Abbot Isaac, whom when we saw close at hand, we addressed with these words.

CHAPTER 4

*Of our return to Abbot Isaac
and question concerning the error
into which the aforesaid old man had fallen*

Although even besides the fresh matter which has lately arisen, our delight in the former conference which was held on the character of prayer would summon us to postpone everything else and return to your holiness, yet this grievous error of Abbot Sarapion, conceived, as we fancy, by the craft of most vile demons, adds somewhat to this desire of ours. For it is no small despair by which we are cast down when we consider that, through the fault of this ignorance, he has not only utterly lost all those labors which he has performed in so praiseworthy a manner for fifty years in this desert, but has also incurred the risk of eternal death. And so we want first to know why and wherefore so grievous an error has crept into him. And next we should like to be taught how we can arrive at that condition in prayer, of which you discoursed some time back not only fully but splendidly. For that admirable Conference has had this effect upon us, that it has only dazzled our minds and has not shown us how to perform or secure it.

CHAPTER 5

The answer on the heresy described above

Is aac: We need not be surprised that a really simple man who had never received any instruction on the substance and nature of the Godhead could still be entangled and deceived by an error of simplicity and the habit of a long-standing mistake and (to speak more truly) continue in the original error which is brought about, not as you suppose by a new illusion of the demons, but by the ignorance of the ancient heathen world, while in accordance with the custom of that erroneous notion, by which they used to worship devils formed in the figure of men, they even now think that the incomprehensible and ineffable glory of the true Deity should be worshipped under the limitations of some figure, as they believe that they can grasp and hold nothing if they have not some image set before them, which they can continually address while they are at their devotions, and which they can carry about in their mind and have always fixed before their eyes.

And against this mistake of theirs this text may be used: "And they changed the glory of the incorruptible God into the likeness of the image of corruptible man" (Romans 1:23). Jeremiah also says: "My people have changed their glory for an idol" (Jeremiah 2:11). Which error although by this its origin, of which we have spoken, it is ingrained in the notions of some, yet none the less is it contracted in the hearts also of those who have never been stained with the superstition of the heathen world, under the color of this passage where it is said, "Let us make man after our image and our likeness" (Genesis 1:26), ignorance and simplicity being its authors, so that actually there has arisen owing to this hateful interpretation a heresy called that of the Anthropomorphites, which maintains with obstinate perverseness that the infinite and simple substance of the Godhead is fashioned in our lineaments and human configuration. Which, however, anyone who has been taught the Catholic doctrine will abhor as heathenish blasphemy, and so will arrive at that perfectly pure condition in prayer which will not only not connect with its prayers any figure of the Godhead or bodily lineaments (which it is a sin even to speak of), but will not even allow in itself even the memory of a name, or the appearance of an action, or an outline of any character.

CHAPTER 6

Of the reasons why Jesus Christ appears to each one of us either in his humility or in his glorified condition

For according to the measure of its purity, as I said in the former Conference, each mind is both raised and molded in its prayers if it forsakes the consideration of earthly and material things so far as the condition of its purity may carry it forward, and enable it with the inner eyes of the soul to see Jesus either still in his humility and in the flesh, or glorified and coming in the glory of his Majesty: for those cannot see Jesus coming in his kingdom who are still kept back in a sort of state of Jewish weakness, and cannot say with the Apostle, "And if we have known Christ after the flesh, yet now we know him so no more" (2 Corinthians 5:16), but only those can look with purest eyes on his Godhead, who rise with him from low and earthly works and thoughts and go apart in the lofty mountain of solitude, which is free from the disturbance of all earthly thoughts and troubles, and secure from the interference of all sins, and being exalted by pure faith and the heights of virtue reveals the glory of his face and the image of his splendor to those who are able to look on him with pure eyes of the soul.

But Jesus is seen as well by those who live in towns and villages and hamlets, i.e., who are occupied in practical affairs and works, but not with the same brightness with which he appeared to those who can go up with him into the aforesaid mount of virtues, i.e., Peter, James, and John. For so in solitude he appeared to Moses and spoke with Elias. And as our Lord wished to establish this and to leave us examples of perfect purity, although he himself, the very fount of inviolable sanctity, had no need of external help and the assistance of solitude in order to secure it (for the fullness of purity could not be soiled by any stain from crowds, nor could he be contaminated by intercourse with men, who cleanses and sanctifies all things that are polluted) yet still he retired into the mountain alone to pray, thus teaching us by the example of his retirement that if we too wish to approach God with a pure and spotless affection of heart, we should also retire from all the disturbance and confusion of crowds, so that while still living in the body we may manage in some degree to adapt ourselves to some likeness of that bliss which is promised hereafter to the saints, and that "God may be" to us "all in all" (1 Corinthians 15:28).

CHAPTER 7
What constitutes our end and perfect bliss

For then will be perfectly fulfilled in our case that prayer of our Savior in which he prayed for his disciples to the Father, saying, "that the love wherewith you loved me may be in them and they in us" (John 17:26), and again, "that they all may be one as you, Father, in me and I in you, that they also may be one in us" (John 17:21), when that perfect love of God, wherewith "he first loved us" (1 John 4:16) has passed into the feelings of our heart as well, by the fulfillment of this prayer of the Lord which we believe cannot possibly be ineffectual. And this will come to pass when God shall be all our love, and every desire and wish and effort, every thought of ours, and all our life and words and breath, and that unity which already exists between the Father and the Son, and the Son and the Father, has been shed abroad in our hearts and minds, so that as he loves us with a pure and unfeigned and indissoluble love, so we also may be joined to him by a lasting and inseparable affection, since we are so united to him that whatever we breathe or think, or speak is God, since, as I say, we attain to that end of which we spoke before, which the same Lord in his prayer hopes may be fulfilled in us: "That they all may be one as we are one, I in them and you in me, that they also may be made perfect in one," and again: "Father, those whom you have given me, I will that where I am, they may also be with me" (John 17:22–24). This, then, ought to be the destination of the solitary, this should be all his aim, that it may be vouchsafed to him to possess even in the body an image of future bliss, and that he may begin in this world to have a foretaste of a sort of earnest of that celestial life and glory. This, I say, is the end of all perfection, that the mind purged from all carnal desires may daily be lifted towards spiritual things, until the whole life and all the thoughts of the heart become one continuous prayer.

CHAPTER 8

A question on the training in perfection by which we can arrive at perpetual recollection of God

GERMANUS: The extent of our bewilderment at our wondering awe at the former Conference, because of which we came back again, increases still more. For in proportion as by the incitements of this teaching we are fired with the desire of perfect bliss, so do we fall back into greater despair, as we know not how to seek or obtain training for such lofty heights. Wherefore we entreat that you will patiently allow us (for it must perhaps be set forth and unfolded with a good deal of talk) to explain what while sitting in the cell we had begun to revolve in a lengthy meditation, although we know that your holiness is not at all troubled by the infirmities of the weak, which even for this reason should be openly set forth, that what is out of place in them may receive correction.

Our notion, then, is that the perfection of any art or system of training must begin with some simple rudiments, and grow accustomed first to somewhat easy and tender beginnings, so that being nourished and trained little by little by a sort of reasonable milk, it may grow up and so by degrees and step by step mount up from the lowest depths to the heights: and when by these means it has entered on the plainer principles and so to speak passed the gates of the entrance of the profession, it will consequently arrive without difficulty at the inmost shrine and lofty heights of perfection. For how could any boy manage to pronounce the simplest union of syllables unless he had first carefully learnt the letters of the alphabet? Or how can any one learn to read quickly, who is still unfit to connect together short and simple sentences? But by what means will one who is ill instructed in the science of grammar attain eloquence in rhetoric or the knowledge of philosophy? Wherefore for this highest learning also, by which we are taught even to cleave to God, I have no doubt that there are some foundations of the system, which must first be firmly laid and afterwards the towering heights of perfection may be placed and raised upon them.

And we have a light idea that these are its first principles, viz., that we should first learn by what meditations God may be grasped and contemplated, and next that we should manage to keep a very firm hold of this topic whatever it is which we do not doubt is the height of all perfection. And therefore we want you to show us some material for this recollection, by which we may conceive and ever keep the idea of God in the mind, so that by always keeping it before our eyes, when we find that we have dropped away from him, we may at once be able to recover ourselves and return thither and may succeed in laying hold of it again without any delay from wandering around the subject and searching for it.

For it happens that when we have wandered away from our spiritual speculations and have come back to ourselves as if waking from a deadly sleep, and, being thoroughly roused, look for the subject matter, by which we may be able to revive that spiritual recollection which has been destroyed, we are hindered by the delay of the actual search before we find it, and are once more drawn aside from our endeavor, and before the spiritual insight is brought about, the purpose of heart which had been conceived has disappeared. And this trouble is certain to happen to us for this reason: because we do not keep something special firmly set before our eyes like some principle to which the wandering thoughts may be recalled after many digressions and varied excursions; and, if I may use the expression, after long storms enter a quiet haven. And so it comes to pass that as the mind is constantly hindered by this want of knowledge and difficulty, and is always tossed about vaguely, and as if intoxicated, among various matters, and cannot even retain firm hold for any length of time of anything spiritual which has occurred to it by chance rather than of set purpose: while, as it is always receiving one thing after another, it does not notice either their beginning and origin or even their end.

CHAPTER 9

The answer on the efficacy of understanding,
which is gained by experience

ISAAC: Your minute and subtle inquiry affords an indication of purity being very nearly reached. For no one would be able even to make inquiries on these matters—I will not say to look within and discriminate—except one who had been urged to sound the depths of such questions by careful and effectual diligence of mind, and watchful anxiety, and one whom the constant aim after a well-controlled life had taught by practical experience to attempt the entrance to this purity and to knock at its doors.

And therefore as I see you, I will not say, standing before the doors of that true prayer of which we have been speaking, but touching its inner chambers and inward parts as it were with the hands of experience, and already laying hold of some parts of it, I do not think that I shall find any difficulty in introducing you now within what I may call its hall, for you to roam about its recesses, as the Lord may direct; nor do I think that you will be hindered from investigating what is to be shown you by any obstacles or difficulties. For he is next door to understanding who carefully recognizes what he ought to ask about, nor is he far from knowledge, who begins to understand how ignorant he is. And therefore I am not afraid of the charge of betraying secrets, and of levity, if I divulge what when speaking in my former discourse on the perfection of prayer I had kept back from discussing, as I think that its force was to be explained to us who are occupied with this subject and interest even without the aid of my words, by the grace of God.

CHAPTER 10

Of the method of continual prayer

Wherefore in accordance with that system, which you admirably compared to teaching children (who can only take in the first lessons on the alphabet and recognize the shapes of the letters, and trace out their characters with a steady hand if they have, by means of some copies and shapes carefully impressed on wax, got accustomed to express their figures, by constantly looking at them and imitating them daily), we must give you also the form of this spiritual contemplation, on which you may always fix your gaze with the utmost steadiness, and both learn to consider it to your profit in unbroken continuance, and also manage by the practice of it and by meditation to climb to a still loftier insight.

This formula, then, shall be proposed to you of this system, which you want, and of prayer, which every monk in his progress towards continual recollection of God, is accustomed to ponder, ceaselessly revolving it in his heart, having got rid of all kinds of other thoughts; for he cannot possibly keep his hold over it unless he has freed himself from all bodily cares and anxieties. And as this was delivered to us by a few of those who were left of the oldest fathers, so it is only divulged by us to a very few and to those who are really keen.

And so, for keeping up continual recollection of God, this pious formula is to be ever set before you: "O God, make speed to save me; O Lord, make haste to help me" (Psalm 70:2). For this verse has not unreasonably been picked out from the whole of Scripture for this purpose. For it embraces all the feelings which can be implanted in human nature, and can be fitly and satisfactorily adapted to every condition, and all assaults. Since it contains an invocation of God against every danger, it contains humble and pious confession, it contains the watchfulness of anxiety and continual fear, it contains the thought of one's own weakness, confidence in the answer, and the assurance of a present and ever ready help. For one who is constantly calling on his protector is certain that he is always at hand. It contains the glow of love and charity, it contains a view of the plots and a dread of the enemies, from which one who sees himself day and night hemmed in by them confesses that he cannot be set free without the aid of his defender.

This verse is an impregnable wall for all who are laboring under the attacks of demons, as well as impenetrable coat of mail and a strong shield. It does not suffer those who are in a state of moroseness and anxiety of mind, or depressed by sadness or all kinds of thoughts to despair of saving remedies, as it shows that he who is invoked is ever looking on at our struggles and is not far from his suppliants. It warns us whose lot is spiritual success and delight of heart that we ought not to be at all elated or puffed up by our happy condition, which it assures us cannot last without God as our protector, while it implores him not only always but even speedily to help us.

This verse, I say, will be found helpful and useful to every one of us in whatever condition we may be. For one who always and in all matters wants to be helped, shows that he needs the assistance of God not only in sorrowful or hard matters but also equally in prosperous and happy ones, that he may be delivered from the one and also made to continue in the other, as he knows that in both of them human weakness is unable to endure without his assistance.

I am affected by the passion of gluttony. I ask for food of which the desert knows nothing, and in the squalid desert there are wafted to me odors of royal dainties, and I find that even against my will I am drawn to long for them. I must at once say: "O God, make speed to save me; O Lord, make haste to help me." I am incited to anticipate the hour fixed for supper, or I am trying with great sorrow of heart to keep to the limits of the right and regular meagre fare. I must cry out with groans: "O God, make speed to save me; O Lord, make haste to help me." Weakness of the stomach hinders me when wanting severer fasts, on account of the assaults of the flesh, or dryness of the belly and constipation frightens me. In order that effect may be given to my wishes, or else that the fire of carnal lust may be quenched without the remedy of a stricter fast, I must pray, "O God, make speed to save me; O Lord, make haste to help me." When I come to supper, at the bidding of the proper hour I loathe taking food and am prevented from eating anything to satisfy the requirements of nature. I must cry with a sigh, "O God, make speed to save me; O Lord, make haste to help me." When I want for the sake of steadfastness of heart to apply myself to reading a headache interferes and stops me, and at the third hour sleep glues my head to the sacred page, and I am forced either to overstep or to anticipate the time assigned to rest; and finally an overpowering desire to sleep forces me to cut short the canonical rule for service in the Psalms. In the same way I must cry out, "O God, make speed to save me; O Lord, make haste to help me." Sleep is withdrawn from my eyes, and for many nights I find myself wearied out with sleeplessness caused by the devil, and all repose and rest by night is kept away from my eyelids. I must sigh and pray, "O God, make speed to save me; O Lord, make haste to help me." While I am still in the midst of a struggle with sin suddenly an irritation of the flesh affects me and tries by a pleasant sensation to draw me to consent while in my sleep. In order that a raging fire from without may not burn up the fragrant blossoms of chastity, I must cry out, "O God, make speed to save me; O Lord, make haste to help me."

I feel that the incentive to lust is removed, and that the heat of passion has died away in my members. In order that this good condition acquired, or rather that this grace of God may continue still longer or forever with me, I must earnestly say, "O God, make speed to save me; O Lord, make haste to help me." I am disturbed by the pangs of anger, covetousness, gloominess, and driven to disturb the peaceful state in which I was, and which was dear to me. In order that I may not be carried away by raging passion into the bitterness of gall, I must cry out with deep groans, "O God, make speed to save me; O Lord, make haste to help me." I am tried by being puffed up by accidie, vainglory, and pride, and my mind with subtle thoughts flatters itself somewhat on account of the coldness and carelessness of others: In order that this dangerous suggestion of the enemy may not get the mastery over me, I must pray with all contrition of heart, "O God, make speed to save me; O Lord, make haste to help me." I have gained the grace of humility and simplicity, and by continually mortifying my spirit have got rid of the swellings of pride: In order that the "foot of pride" may not again "come against me," and "the hand of the sinner disturb me" (Psalm 36:12), and that I may not be more seriously damaged by elation at my success, I must cry with all my might, "O God, make speed to save me; O Lord, make haste to help me."

I am on fire with innumerable and various wanderings of soul and shiftiness of heart, and cannot collect my scattered thoughts, nor can I even pour forth my prayer without interruption and images of vain figures, and the recollection of conversations and actions, and I feel myself tied down by such dryness and barrenness that I feel I cannot give birth to any offspring in the shape of spiritual ideas. In order that it may be vouchsafed to me to be set free from this wretched state of mind, from which I cannot extricate myself by any number of sighs and groans, I must full surely cry out, "O God, make speed to save me; O Lord, make haste to help me."

Again, I feel that by the visitation of the Holy Spirit I have gained purpose of soul, steadfastness of thought, keenness of heart, together with an ineffable joy and transport of mind, and in the exuberance of spiritual feelings I have perceived by a sudden illumination from the Lord an abounding revelation of most holy ideas which were formerly altogether hidden from me. In order that it may be vouchsafed to me to linger for a longer time in them I must often and anxiously exclaim, "O God, make speed to save me; O Lord, make haste to help me." Encompassed by nightly horrors of devils I am agitated, and am disturbed by the appearances of unclean spirits, my very hope of life and salvation is withdrawn by the horror of fear. Flying to the safe refuge of this verse, I will cry out with all my might, "O God, make speed to save me; O Lord, make haste to help me." Again, when I have been restored by the Lord's consolation, and, cheered by his coming, feel myself encompassed as if by countless thousands of angels, so that all of a sudden I can venture to seek the conflict and provoke a battle with those whom a while ago I dreaded worse than death, and whose touch or even approach I felt with a shudder both of mind and body. In order that the vigor of this courage may, by God's grace, continue in me still longer, I must cry out with all my powers, "O God, make speed to save me; O Lord, make haste to help me."

We must, then, ceaselessly and continuously pour forth the prayer of this verse, in adversity that we may be delivered, in prosperity that we may be preserved and not puffed up. Let the thought of this verse, I tell you, be meditated over in your breast without ceasing. Whatever work you are doing, or office you are holding, or journey you are going, do not cease to chant this. When you are going to bed, or eating, and in the last necessities of nature, think on this. This thought in your heart may be to you a saving formula, and not only keep you unharmed by all attacks of devils, but also purify you from all faults and earthly stains, and lead you to that invisible and celestial contemplation, and carry you on to that ineffable glow of prayer, of which so few have any experience. Let sleep come upon you still considering this verse, till having been molded by the constant use of it, you grow accustomed to repeat it even in your sleep. When you wake let it be the first thing to come into your mind, let it anticipate all your waking thoughts, let it when you rise from your bed send you down on your knees, and thence send you forth to all your work and business, and let it follow you about all day long. This you should think about, according to the Lawgiver's charge, "at home and walking forth on a journey" (Deuteronomy 6:7), sleeping and waking. This you should write on the threshold and door of your mouth, this you should place on the walls of your house and in the recesses of your heart so that when you fall on your knees in prayer this may be your chant as you kneel, and when you rise up from it to go forth to all the necessary business of life it may be your constant prayer as you stand.

CHAPTER 11
Of the perfection of prayer
to which we can rise by the system described

This, this is the formula which the mind should unceasingly cling to until, strengthened by the constant use of it and by continual meditation, it casts off and rejects the rich and full material of all manner of thoughts, and restricts itself to the poverty of this one verse, and so arrives with ready ease at that beatitude of the gospel, which holds the first place among the other beatitudes: for he says "Blessed are the poor in spirit, for theirs is the kingdom of heaven" (Matthew 5:3). And so one who becomes grandly poor by a poverty of this sort will fulfill this saying of the prophet: "The poor and needy shall praise the name of the Lord." (Psalm 74:21). And indeed what greater or holier poverty can there be than that of one who knowing that he has no defence and no strength of his own, asks for daily help from another's bounty, and as he is aware that every single moment his life and substance depend on divine assistance, professes himself not without reason the Lord's almsman, and cries to him daily in prayer: "But I am poor and needy: the Lord helps me" (Psalm 40:17).

And so, by the illumination of God himself, he mounts to that manifold knowledge of him and begins henceforward to be nourished on sublimer and still more sacred mysteries, in accordance with these words of the prophet: "The high hills are a refuge for the stags, the rocks for the hedgehogs" (Psalm 104:18), which is very fairly applied in the sense we have given because whosoever continues in simplicity and innocence is not injurious or offensive to anyone, but being content with his own simple condition endeavors simply to defend himself from being spoiled by his foes, and becomes a sort of spiritual hedgehog and is protected by the continual shield of that rock of the gospel, i.e., being sheltered by the recollection of the Lord's passion and by ceaseless meditation on the verse given above he escapes the snares of his opposing enemies. And of these spiritual hedgehogs we read in Proverbs as follows: "And the

hedgehogs are a feeble folk, who have made their homes in the rocks"
(Proverbs 30:26). And indeed what is feebler than a Christian, what is
weaker than a monk, who is not only not permitted any vengeance for
wrongs done to him but is actually not allowed to suffer even a slight
and silent feeling of irritation to spring up within?

But whoever advances from this condition and not only secures the
simplicity of innocence, but is also shielded by the virtue of discretion,
becomes an exterminator of deadly serpents, and has Satan crushed
beneath his feet, and by his quickness of mind answers to the figure of
the reasonable stag, this man will feed on the mountains of the prophets
and Apostles, i.e., on their highest and loftiest mysteries. And thriving
on this pasture continually, he will take in to himself all the thoughts of
the Psalms, and will begin to sing them in such a way that he will utter
them with the deepest emotion of heart not as if they were the composi-
tions of the Psalmist, but rather as if they were his own utterances and
his very own prayer; and will certainly take them as aimed at himself,
and will recognize that their words were not only fulfilled formerly by
or in the person of the prophet, but that they are fulfilled and carried
out daily in his own case.

For then the Holy Scriptures lie open to us with greater clearness
and, as it were, their very veins and marrow are exposed, when our
experience not only perceives but actually anticipates their meaning,
and the sense of the words is revealed to us not by an exposition of them
but by practical proof. For if we have experience of the very state of
mind in which each Psalm was sung and written, we become like their
authors and anticipate the meaning rather than follow it, i.e., gathering
the force of the words before we really know them, we remember what
has happened to us, and what is happening in daily assaults when the
thoughts of them come over us, and while we sing them we call to mind
all that our carelessness has brought upon us, or our earnestness has
secured, or Divine Providence has granted or the promptings of the foe
have deprived us of, or slippery and subtle forgetfulness has carried off,
or human weakness has brought about, or thoughtless ignorance has

cheated us of. For all these feelings we find expressed in the Psalms, so that by seeing whatever happens as in a very clear mirror, we understand it better, and so instructed by our feelings as our teachers we lay hold of it as something not merely heard but actually seen, and, as if it were not committed to memory, but implanted in the very nature of things, we are affected from the very bottom of the heart, so that we get at its meaning not by reading the text but by experience anticipating it. And so our mind will reach that incorruptible prayer to which in our former treatise, as the Lord vouchsafed to grant, the scheme of our Conference mounted, and this is not merely not engaged in gazing on any image, but is actually distinguished by the use of no words or utterances; but with the purpose of the mind all on fire, is produced through ecstasy of heart by some unaccountable keenness of spirit, and the mind being thus affected without the aid of the senses or any visible material pours it forth to God with groanings and sighs that cannot be uttered.

CHAPTER 12

A question as to how spiritual thoughts
can be retained without losing them

GERMANUS: We think that you have described to us not only the system of this spiritual discipline for which we asked, but perfection itself; and this with great clearness and openness. For what can be more perfect and sublime than for the recollection of God to be embraced in so brief a meditation, and for it, dwelling on a single verse, to escape from all the limitations of things visible, and to comprise in one short word the thoughts of all our prayers. And therefore we beg you to explain to us one thing which still remains, viz., how we can keep firm hold of this verse which you have given us as a formula, in such a way that, as we have been by God's grace set free from the trifles of worldly thoughts, so we may also keep a steady grasp on all spiritual ones.

CHAPTER 13
On the lightness of thoughts

For when the mind has taken in the meaning of a passage in any Psalm, this insensibly slips away from it, and ignorantly and thoughtlessly it passes on to a text of some other Scripture. And when it has begun to consider this with itself, while it is still not thoroughly explored, the recollection of some other passage springs up, and shuts out the consideration of the former subject. From this too it is transferred to some other, by the entrance of some fresh consideration, and the soul always turns about from Psalm to Psalm and jumps from a passage in the Gospels to read one in the Epistles, and from this passes on to the prophetic writings, and thence is carried to some spiritual history, and so it wanders about vaguely and uncertainly through the whole body of the Scriptures, unable, as it may choose, either to reject or keep hold of anything, or to finish anything by fully considering and examining it, and so becomes only a toucher or taster of spiritual meanings, not an author and possessor of them. And so the mind, as it is always light and wandering, is distracted even in time of service by all sorts of things, as if it were intoxicated, and does not perform any office properly.

For instance, while it is praying, it is recalling some Psalm or passage of Scripture. While it is chanting, it is thinking about something else besides what the text of the Psalm itself contains. When it repeats a passage of Scripture, it is thinking about something that has to be done, or remembering something that has been done. And in this way it takes in and rejects nothing in a disciplined and proper way, and seems to be driven about by random incursions, without the power either of retaining what it likes or lingering over it. It is then well for us before everything else to know how we can properly perform these spiritual offices, and keep firm hold of this particular verse which you have given us as a formula, so that the rise and fall of our feelings may not be in a state of fluctuation from their own lightness, but may lie under our own control.

CHAPTER 14

The answer how we can gain
stability of heart or of thoughts

ISAAC: Although, in our former discussion on the character of prayer,
enough was, as I think, said on this subject, yet as you want it repeated
to you again, I will give you a brief instruction on steadfastness of heart.
There are three things which make a shifting heart steadfast—watchings,
meditation, and prayer—diligence in which, and constant attention,
will produce steadfast firmness of mind. But this cannot be secured
in any other way unless all cares and anxieties of this present life have
been first got rid of by indefatigable persistence in work dedicated not
to covetousness but to the sacred uses of the monastery, that we may
thus be able to fulfil the Apostle's command, "Pray without ceasing" (1
Thessalonians 5:17). For he prays too little, who is accustomed only to
pray at the times when he bends his knees. But he never prays, who even
while on his bended knees is distracted by all kinds of wanderings of
heart. And therefore what we would be found when at our prayers, that
we ought to be before the time of prayer. For at the time of its prayers,
the mind cannot help being affected by its previous condition, and while
it is praying, will be either transported to things heavenly, or dragged
down to earthly things by those thoughts in which it had been lingering
before prayer.

Thus far did Abbot Isaac carry on his Second Conference on the character
of prayer to us astonished hearers; whose instruction on the consideration of that verse quoted above (which he gave as a sort of outline for
beginners to hold) we greatly admired, and wished to follow very closely,
as we fancied that it would be a short and easy method; but we have
found it even harder to observe than that system of ours by which we
used formerly to wander here and there in varied meditations through
the whole body of the Scriptures without being tied by any chains of
perseverance. It is, then, certain that no one is kept away from perfection

of heart by not being able to read, nor is rustic simplicity any hindrance to the possession of purity of heart and mind, which lies close at hand for all, if only they will by constant meditation on this verse keep the thoughts of the mind safe and sound towards God.

CPSIA information can be obtained at www.ICGtesting.com
Printed in the USA
LVOW01s0300160715

446356LV00032B/985/P